LIGHTING THE WAY

Dear Uncle Don & Aunt Marge,

May God continue to Bless your family for Our Lord Jesus Christ.

Love + prayers,
Mary
I Thes 5:18
August, 2000

LIGHTING THE WAY

A 90-Day Journey in Sharing Your Faith

Mary Marr
Radio Host of *Outreach Alert*

Beacon Hill Press of Kansas City
Kansas City, Missouri

Copyright 2000
By Beacon Hill Press of Kansas City

ISBN 083-411-8408

Printed in the United States of America

Cover Design by Mike Walsh

Library of Congress Control Number: 00-058506

10   9   8   7   6   5   4   3   2   1

Contents

Introduction

Welcome to *Lighting the Way,* a spiritual journey to share your faith in Jesus Christ effectively and to become a fully functioning Lighthouse in just 90 days!

Lighting the Way is designed to complement the growing national Mission America Lighthouse Movement, bringing together over 450 Christian leaders who represent 90+ denominations and some 350 ministries for the Great Commission. In January 1999 the Mission America coalition of leaders launched the Lighthouse Movement to help mobilize the church to pray for, care for, and share Christ with every person in America.

A Lighthouse is a person, family, church, or any group of people who commit to pray and care for those in their network of friends and family and then sensitively share Jesus Christ with them as God directs.

Your *Lighting the Way* workbook is designed for use individually or with a group of professed believers who meet regularly and are committed to growth in witnessing. As you pray together for the unsaved persons God has placed in your path, you will also pray for each other to grow in sharing your faith in Christ more effectively. Any Sunday School class or small group may use *Lighting the Way* by taking 10 minutes of a regular class session to discuss the week's steps, review new skills, and hold each other accountable for witnessing growth in the prayer, care, and share areas.

Definitions

For our purposes, we will define *sharing* as any method, activity, or principle that seeks to introduce the gospel, challenge, and follow up with new or growing believers. God has gifted some people with a special gift to bring others to a saving knowledge of Jesus Christ as personal Lord and Savior. Some are personal evangelists and some are large event proclamation evangelists, such as Dr. Billy Graham.

Witnessing is sharing with others what we know and have experienced as believers person-

ally in our relationship with Jesus Christ. While we may not all have the gift of the evangelist, 2 Tim. 4:5 calls all of us to "do the work of an evangelist." God has uniquely gifted each one of us with special traits to expand His kingdom. These may be gifts of mercy, hospitality, teaching, administration, or service. Whatever our gifts from God, we are all called to give an account of our personal experience with Christ in such a way that the Great Commission (Matt. 28:19-20) may be fulfilled. The Great Commission is not a choice but a command for the committed, obedient, and mature follower of Jesus Christ. There are no gray areas concerning this command.

Goal

The goal of the *Lighting the Way* workbook is to guide Christians who are not actively sharing their faith into fully functioning witnesses of Christ's transforming power. Some may have witnessing experience but feel ineffective due to lack of basic skills. Some may have basic skills but may not have submitted to an accountability structure to ensure effective use. However, many Christians do not have any background in this spiritual discipleship area.

Regardless of your background, there are three factors that will ensure your success in *Lighting the Way.*

Success Factors

The successful usage of the *Lighting the Way* workbook depends upon these three factors:

1. the seriousness of your commitment to use the study in its step-by-step design
2. the faithfulness of your commitment to apply the prayer, care, share daily guidelines
3. the strength of your accountability relationship to ensure this becomes a natural part of your life

While such habits as tithing, prayer, worship, and Bible study may be part of our routine as believers, often sharing our faith has been left out. God himself has asked that we grow in this area in obedience to Him, and the *Lighting the Way* workbook will help you.

You have taken the first and hardest step. God will reward your obedience in developing an effective prayer, care, and share lifestyle. Sharing Christ is not an art, but a decision.

You have decided to follow the command of Our Lord. Congratulations!

How to Use *Lighting the Way*

Weekly Design

You can be fully functioning as a Lighthouse in one week. You can be an effective Lighthouse in 30 days.

Each page of the 90-day journey is designed to take you in sequential steps toward more effective witnessing. Each day offers a challenge question, scripture verse, discussion, and inspiration, as well as specific guidelines to exercise prayer, care, and share (PCS) responses. Each week concludes with a review section to log your responses to the daily exercises followed by a chart to log your progress. The progress chart is designed for you to fill in a PCS action idea.

If after 90 days your seekers have not made a personal commitment to Jesus Christ, you may choose to start over with Week 1, Day 1 or at any point you feel the sharing process has stalled.

Accountability Partners

At the end of each week you will connect with your accountability prayer partner for personal growth insights, review of PCS progress, along with specific prayer requests for those God has placed on your heart. Your accountability partner needs to be someone you see on a regular basis—a person who is committed to witnessing growth, will hold you accountable for growth, is mature and holy in his or her walk with Christ, and whose prayer life you have confidence in. Start praying now for God to lead you into this relationship, which is vital to effective witnessing. Place the name, address, and telephone number of your accountability partner in the front of your workbook. You might even want to record the date you and your partner begin praying for each other.

Seekers

In week 1 you will prayerfully record the names of three to five people to whom God is leading you to share His love in your current daily relationships. Do not proceed with the next week PCS action guidelines until you have created your list of three to five people. While you may feel more strongly about some individuals on your list than others, it is important to allow God to lead you in the selection process. God will often unexpectedly give us a tender heart for a person. Log the names, addresses, and telephone numbers of your three to five seekers at the front of your workbook.

While this study is designed to fit many common steps to sharing, your seeker may be ready to move to receiving the gospel earlier than this series provides. In that case, move directly to the share section and begin that process.

Review Summary

Each weekday you will be directed to answer three questions related to the text. Answer these questions in the space provided on the day 6 review summary. When you meet weekly with your accountability partner you will share your summary answers as well as your action steps from Charting My Course on Day 7.

Charting My Course

You will apply the PCS action guidelines with your three to five seekers throughout the 90-day journey. Each day the PCS guidelines will reflect the topic highlighted and will become more in-depth as you go through the book. Each section will have a primary PCS emphasis. Each daily PCS works together to lead up to six weeks of praying, caring, and sharing actions, followed by exercising direct sharing action steps. You may choose to implement the suggested PCS guideline for each day, or you may choose one of your own. Charting My Course will form a comprehensive strategy as you fill in PCS actions for each week. Each day you will move closer to helping those on your prayer list make a decision to follow Christ as Lord and Savior.

You will want to move through each section as quickly as possible. You must develop a sense of urgency in the salvation of others, for we never know how much time each person has left. However, if for some reason you have had to stop the process, through illness, for example, do not move to the next week until you have thoroughly applied the PCS action guidelines.

Appendixes

Familiarize yourself with the various topics covered in the appendixes. You will be using these pages with frequency throughout your 90-day journey. These sections offer many useful materials pertinent to sharing the gospel.

Prayer, Care, Share Ideas. The Prayer List, Care List, and Share List (Appendixes A, B, and C) offer sequential or random ideas for each area. When completing your daily reading, you may select ideas from these lists or use ideas of your own. You will be prompted to add your ideas to the PCS lists for each of the names on your unsaved prayer list. You may elect to carry over a PCS idea to the following week. At the end of each week you will select from your lists of ideas a next action step for each person on your list. Only you will know where each person is on the spiritual growth continuum.

Resources. At the back of this book is a list of recommended resources (Appendix J) for you to draw from throughout your 90-day journey.

This section will help you find more in-depth materials for ongoing reference in your Lighthouse lifestyle. You will find these tools helpful in sharing prior to your seeker's conversion and immediately afterward. You are not alone in your 90-day journey. God is with you and your prayer partner, and I am just an E-mail away to answer any question, big or small.

Remember, your goal is not the conversion of your seekers. God is responsible for that. Your goal is the witnessing process of sharing what you know and have experienced with one who does not know or follow Jesus. You no longer have to carry around guilt for the unsaved when you are doing your part. Think about it this way—your part God *will not* do, His part you *cannot* do.

Leader's Guide. The leader's guide (Appendix K) offers those directing the weekly review or accountability session additional tips on using the *Lighting the Way* material. The guide is useful for preparing, focusing, and determining the progress of participants. Additional material and answers to questions may be found at the Outreach Alert web site at <www.outreachalert.org>.

Week 1—A Searching Lighthouse

DAY 1

Challenge Question—Why should we become a praying, caring, sharing Lighthouse?

Read—1 Tim. 2:1-8

Action Item—Define God's desire for you as stated in verse 4.

Our desire to become a Lighthouse comes from our desire to be obedient to Christ. The Great Commission (Matt. 28:19-20) is not a choice. We were saved to disciple both globally and locally. Jesus came to redeem not only our families but also the world. We are His means for reaching the lost. Jesus stayed focused on God, not on needs, when He walked among us. This focus allowed Him to do God's will. He reached us because He was strong in His own relationship with God. When we are on our knees for the lost, we, too, will be effective witnesses for God.

God cared enough to give us His very best model of sharing the Good News—Jesus. And He admonished us to tend His lambs, shepherd His sheep, and follow Him (John 21:15-19). That means we are to take the Word of God to believers and nonbelievers alike. These commands of evangelism, discipleship, shepherding, and obedient worship give us a healthy plan for building followers of Christ. Being a Lighthouse allows us to lead those who are being tossed to and fro on the sea of life to the safe harbor of Christ. When we pray, care, and share as Jesus did, we may become the only Jesus some will ever know (Phil. 2:8-11).

Prayer—Thank God right now for your own salvation and the one who brought you the Good News.

Care—With a heart of love toward our Lord and Savior, commit to give your time to carefully completing *Lighting the Way*.

Share—Share with another believer how you have just committed to completing the 90-day Lighthouse journey to witness effectively.

Sail on Over to Day 6—Complete questions 1-3 of the review summary for day 6.

Charting My Course on Day 7—Based on today's reading, alter or add to your plan of action by charting your course on day 7 as described in the introduction in Seekers and Charting My Course.

Thought for the Day—When we are on our knees for the lost, we, too, will be effective witnesses for God.

DAY 2

Challenge Question—What will happen if I do not pray for and care for the lost and share Christ?

Read—1 Tim. 2:1-8

Action Item—Highlight the benefits of prayer as mentioned in verse 2.

What will happen if we do not share Christ with the lost? They will die an eternal death, God will be broken-hearted, and we will never experience the exhilaration, joy, and fulfillment of obeying God in His plan for the world. We will face eternal consequences, and evil will continue its destructive course in the lives of those who don't know God.

Since Jesus walked the earth and proclaimed the truth to set humanity free, His disciples have continued to do likewise. If you are not moved by the plight of the lost, those without a personal relationship with Jesus, you have moved beyond the guilt stage into a worse condition—dreaded complacency. You and I will give an account for the stewardship of our God-given time. We are accountable to share what He has given us, and the consequence of our disobedience is immeasurable.

Winning the lost to Christ makes us world-changers. It provides an adventure with God that draws us closer to Him in every way. Pleasing God by praying for, caring for, and sharing the gospel with others will bring us the greatest level of satisfaction we will ever know.

Prayer—Ask God to search your heart for any disobedience in bringing the gospel to the unsaved. Ask God to melt your heart for the lost He has placed in your path.

Care—Begin today to be a responsible, obedient Lighthouse who honors God.

Share—Confess to God the areas you have let slide in being an obedient Lighthouse. Tell God what you intend to do about any disobedience.

Sail on Over to Day 6—Complete questions 4-6 of the review summary for day 6.

Charting My Course on Day 7—Based on today's reading, alter or add to your plan of action by charting your course on day 7.

Thought for the Day—Pleasing God by praying for, caring for, and sharing the gospel with others will bring us the greatest level of satisfaction we will ever know.

DAY 3

Challenge Question—Who is searching for God?
Reread—1 Tim. 2:1-8
Action Item—Memorize 1 Tim. 2:1.

First Timothy reminds us that all who are lost need to be saved. Everyone without Christ needs to know of His love. All people seek God whether or not they confess it. Thousands of people profess to be perfectly happy without Christ. So, where is the problem?

Jesus came to bring peace, not superficial happiness. Before we can be effective witnesses we must see the real needs of the people around us, and only the Holy Spirit can show us each individual's unique needs. Until we discover through the help of the Holy Spirit what the root of the needs are for the unsaved, our witness will not penetrate their souls. Common needs are peace, purpose, joy, truth, security, forgiveness, or significance. Our responsibility is to discover the pressing needs of the unsaved.

Most people can easily tell you where they are emotionally, physically, intellectually, or socially. However, many have never verbalized their spiritual state. Just ask an unsaved person how you can pray for him or her. Usually that simple request will reveal the person's deep needs from a spiritual perspective. Most people will be glad you cared enough to ask the question. Very rarely will someone refuse your prayer. You may have to clarify the response into a direct need category or a biblically sound request. Yet once you help formulate the requests and needs, commit to pray regularly for each one by name. Then regularly follow up on the results. At the very least you will build a bridge for having further spiritual conversations. Don't be fooled into believing that your unsaved friends do not have spiritual needs.

Prayer—Pray that God will help you discover the spiritual needs of the unsaved people around you.

Care—Review the Care List (Appendix B). Think of additional care ideas that fit your unique gifts.

Share—Ask where one person is in his or her personal spiritual journey and share by simply listening.

Sail on Over to Day 6—Complete questions 7-9 of the review summary for day 6.

Charting My Course on Day 7—Based on today's reading, alter or add to your plan of action by charting your course on day 7.

Thought for the Day—All people seek God whether or not they confess it.

DAY 4

Challenge Question—Where can God use me?

Reread—1 Tim. 2:1-8

God has providentially placed people in our path with whom He wants us to share His Son. While praying for strangers is important for this exercise, you are asked to seek God's direction in guiding you to people you see regularly. It could be your son's coach, a family member, a friend, a barber, a clerk, or a neighbor. Think through your weekly schedule and write down 10 names of people with whom you routinely interact. Then ask God to impress upon you 3 to 5 people for whom you should pray each day during your 90-day journey.

Choose an accountability prayer partner from among your contacts at church, in Sunday School, within your family, or among Christian friends. Your prayer partner needs to have the same commitment you have to pray for, care for, and share Christ more effectively within the next three months. This person should be someone in your sphere of influence with whom you meet regularly and already have a common ground. This will help you avoid having to make additional time commitments. Remember, this should be fun and not be viewed as another obligation.

List 10 names of unbelievers for whom you will begin praying:

_____

_____

_____

_____

_____

_____

_____

_____

_____

_____

Prayer—Pause and ask God to confirm the names of people He has placed in your path who need a personal relationship with Jesus Christ.

Care—Add specific ideas to the Care List (Appendix B) that may meet the needs of those God has placed on your heart.

Share—Share with your accountability prayer partner the names God has laid on your heart.

Sail on Over to Day 6—Complete questions 10-12 of the review summary for day 6.

Charting My Course on Day 7—Record the names of the three to five people on your chart. Fill in the next steps of prayer, care, share actions from the lists in Appendixes A, B, and C.

Thought for the Day—God has providentially placed people in our path with whom He wants us to share His Son.

DAY 5

Challenge Question—Is God giving me a burden?
Action Item—Quote out loud 1 Tim. 2:1.

As you continue to pray over the names on your prayer list, God will soften your heart for each one. You will soon be able to empathize and feel deep understanding and compassion for them all. Why? Because Jesus is faithful and you have asked Him to make you sensitive to the needs of others. Each time you see a person on your prayer list you will feel a special blessing because you and God are on a special mission of love.

As you pray for God's help to see each person's needs clearly, you will begin to see his or her unique needs physically, vocationally, emotionally, mentally, socially, and spiritually. Remember that not every problem a person has will be spiritual, but it will have a spiritual dimension. For example, someone who is mentally handicapped has a mental capacity problem. He or she may also need spiritual growth help but ultimately has a mental problem.

Do not confuse problems with needs. Often true needs are met prior to conversion. Mental and emotional problems can sometimes run hand in hand with spiritual maturity. Physical problems may hinder some from attending church. Social problems may cause some to restrict their vulnerability by refusing to reveal *any* problems. Vocational problems may cause some to hold back in making godly lifestyle choices. Nowhere in Scripture does God promise to answer the prayers of the unrighteous, but He does delight in meeting needs that will lead to salvation. Talk to God about the burdens of those on your prayer list.

Prayer—Pray for God to fill your heart with compassion and help you to understand the difference between the spiritual needs and the problems facing those on your prayer list.

Care—Select one care idea from the Care List (Appendix B) to implement today.

Share—Ask your accountability prayer partner to pray that your care action would take root deeply in the hearts of those on your prayer list.

Sail on Over to Day 6—Complete questions 13-15 of the review summary for day 6.

Charting My Course on Day 7—Record the prayer, care, share steps necessary for each of your seekers for next week. Thank God for what He has done through you this week.

Thought for the Day—Ed Silvoso, from Harvest Evangelism, says: "Talk to God about your neighbor, before you talk to your neighbor about God" (*Lighthouse Movement Handbook*, 23).

Congratulations—you are now a fully functioning Lighthouse!

DAY 6

Review Summary

Prayer, Care, and Share

On each of the 90 days you will be prompted to complete a prayer, care, and share activity. The goal is to focus on five people throughout the study. After prayerfully considering which five people God wants you to direct your prayer, care, and share energy toward, write down their names here:

1. _____
2. _____
3. _____
4. _____
5. _____

As you think of these people, make a care and share possibility list below. What acts of kindness, encouragement, help, and friendship could you use in reaching these people for Christ? See Appendixes A, B, and C, then add your own ideas to this list:

- Collect cards and notes for quick sending.
- Plan a quick meal you could share with one of the families.
- Use a two-for-one coupon and share the extra with someone.
- Share a family activity.
- Get your family to help in offering baby-sitting or yard care during a busy time.
- Find out where your life and the lives of those on your list already overlap because of common involvements, and offer transportation to an event.

Questions 1-15

1. What does God want us to do with our salvation?

2. What do you think the word *co-mission* means?

3. How did Jesus model prayer, care, and share?

4. What will be the consequences if we do not witness?

5. Are you being moved by the plight of people who are without the peace of God?

6. What are some of the advantages you will have by being obedient to God in sharing your faith?

7. In what ways are people pretending they do not need God?

8. Who is the only one who can show us the real needs of the unsaved?

9. What happened when you asked one unsaved person where he or she was regarding a personal spiritual journey?

10. Identify the names of 10 people you see regularly.

11. Identify those on the list with whom you have a common ground (i.e., son's coach, family).

12. Identify the names of three to five people God has been impressing upon you to pray for, care for, and share Christ within the next 90 days.

13. Why is it important to talk to God about those on your prayer list before witnessing to them?

14. What concerns does God have for those on your prayer list? Be specific.

15. What are the needs God is showing you for your seekers? How can you be supportive in getting help for problems that may distract them from pursuing their true spiritual needs?

DAY 7

Charting My Course

Based on this week's readings, alter or add to your plan of action by charting your course.

	Name	Prayer Action	Care Action	Share Action	Prayer Answer
Day 1					
Day 2					
Day 3					
Day 4					
Day 5					
Day 6					
Day 7					

Week 2—A Radiating Lighthouse

DAY 1

Challenge Question—What do I need to do to get ready?

Read—John 17:13-21

Action Item—Define the phrase *personal prayer reward.*

In order to prepare to share God's love you need to pray, pray, and then pray some more. We can all pray for the unsaved. We do not have to have the gift of evangelism to offer the prayer of the evangelist. We can all thank God for our salvation and then ask Him to use us to pass on that blessing. We can all experience the joy and exhilaration that comes from a holy, fervent prayer for someone in need. Just as we get our homes ready for guests during the holidays by cleaning windows or polishing silver, our personal prayers for the lost are as effective in preparing us to share God's love as the cleanliness of our walk with Christ. Fervent and righteous prayers are productive.

Are you a model of Jesus in daily prayer, thankfulness, peacefulness, holiness, faith, obedience, service, and love? How thankful you are for your own salvation will largely determine your passion in sharing it with others. Your intense expression of deep concern to God on behalf of seekers comes from your love of God and His children. Fervent praying brings you into agreement with a holy and loving God and enables you to respond to seekers as He would.

Prayer—Thank God for the fullness of joy He has given you today. Bring your seekers' requests to the Lord.

Care—Look for a newspaper or magazine article on a topic of interest to your unsaved friend.

Share—When your friend thanks you for being so thoughtful to share the article, mention that it is Jesus who helps you be thoughtful or kind.

Sail on Over to Day 6—Complete questions 1-3 of the review summary for day 6.

Charting My Course on Day 7—Based on today's reading, alter or add to your plan of action by charting your course on day 7.

Thought for the Day—How thankful you are for your own salvation will largely determine your passion in sharing it with others.

DAY 2

Challenge Question—Where can I get prayer power?
Recite—John 17:21
Action Item—Define the phrase *all may be one.*

Acts 1:8 says we will be His witnesses when the Holy Spirit comes upon us. Praying for boldness and confidence when witnessing is vital (4:29).

When we pray, God will give us faith that overcomes all fear and the temptation to avoid sharing what God has done in us. By praying we keep His goals at the forefront of our minds, and He gives us courage beyond ourselves. Total heart abandonment to God is the key.

When we exhibit the peace that passes all understanding, the world sits up and takes notice that our reason for inner peace and doing what is right comes from God. For example, when we return the incorrect change at the store, who receives the honor for all to see? And when we reverently bow to offer a prayer of thanks in a restaurant, who sees the honored unseen Guest at our table? The gospel does not come in word only, but in power through the Holy Spirit. For believers, prayer sustains our walk as imitators of Christ, proving what kind of disciples we are to a turbulent world. Prayer is the beginning, sustaining, purifying, empowering, and unifying means that "all may be one" with God and that they would believe in Him. Praying for seekers makes them aware of their sin and unsettles their spiritual status quo.

Prayer—Ask the Holy Spirit to fill your heart with His love, boldness, confidence, and perseverance to share the gospel with those on your prayer list.

Care—Offer to help someone on your prayer list with a difficult household task. This will demonstrate a loving action to a genuine seeker.

Share—When this person asks you why you are going out of your way to help, let him or her know God has prompted you to help. Be sure to give Him the credit in some way.

Sail on Over to Day 6—Complete questions 4-6 of the review summary for day 6.

Charting My Course on Day 7—Based on today's reading, alter or add to your plan of action by charting your course on day 7.

Thought for the Day—The gospel does not come in word only, but in power through the Holy Spirit.

DAY 3

Challenge Question—Who should I pray with?
Read—John 17:14-16
Action Item—Define the term *disciple*.

Salvation without obedience is dead, just as faith without works is dead. In selecting an accountability partner for this study you need to choose someone you will see on a regular basis—a person who is committed to witnessing growth, will hold you accountable for growth, is mature and holy in his or her walk with Christ, and whose prayer life you have confidence in. If you have already selected an accountability partner, discuss these responsibilities together.

When we accepted Christ as personal Savior, we made a lifetime commitment to follow Him as Lord over every area of our life. Our accountability partner should share our convictions. Remember, the fervent prayers of a righteous person will produce fruit. Your selection of an accountability partner in prayer is essential. While you may enjoy his or her fellowship and friendship, the ultimate test is this person's walk with God and ability to love you enough to want to see you grow in your faith and Christian witness. Just like parents, accountability partners do not do us any favors by being either overly lenient or overly strict. Only God can help determine the difference. Appropriate challenge, when tempered with appropriate understanding, provides a healthy balance for long-term growth in witnessing. For example, athletic coaches know that scouting to build a winning team is worth the time and effort.

Disciples who are set apart from worldly influence (pure in attitude and lifestyle choices), grounded in the truth, and tested in perseverance under attack will make a winning witnessing team.

Prayer—Thank God for the accountability prayer partner He has given you. Ask God to grant your seekers the spiritual desires of their hearts.
Care—Look for one wholesome trait in the lives of each person on your prayer list and find a way to affirm his or her goodness in that area.
Share—Tell those on your prayer list you thank God for giving them these character traits because you know these traits come from Him.

Sail on Over to Day 6—Complete questions 7-9 of the review summary for day 6.

Charting My Course on Day 7—Based on today's reading, alter or add to your plan of action by charting your course on day 7.

Thought for the Day—The fervent prayers of the righteous will produce fruit.

DAY 4

Challenge Question—Why must prayers be unhindered?
Read—John 17:15-19
Action Item—Define the term *sanctify*.

Dr. Charles Stanley once said, "If we are not a praying people, we are a defeated people. Prayer is not me motivating God to save my family member or friend; it is me being motivated to do my part." Prayer is God's motivational channel in our lives. Just as the TV remote is used to change the channel, we can tune this motivational channel in or out.

In addition to motivational challenges, sometimes we are tempted to play the "if only" game: "If only I had more time; if only I did not have to work; if only I did not have this illness." Our "if onlys" hinder God's plan for our work in the lives of others. Paul, in Acts 23, viewed his "if only" disappointments as God's footholds for sharing the gospel. He made a choice to travel an obedient path.

Where does this darkness, discouragement, and disappointment come from? The devil. However, Jesus fought the forces of evil and won! Now we as Christians can be victors in the world and not be dragged down by it. We may be tempted on every side, but not destroyed, when our lives are sanctified fully unto Him. Just as the disciples in Acts 4:31 stood firm in their convictions regarding sin, we, too, are given this same power to stand firm by the Holy Spirit.

We must be close to God when life's challenges come. If we are not close enough to God to withstand persecution when it comes, who is it that has moved in our relationship with Him? We must place God first in our priorities. The fate of Ananias and Sapphira was death for being dishonest with God. However, when obedience reigned, the whole Church was shaken up and multitudes were saved. We are witnesses to the powerful sanctifying work of Jesus Christ for one reason: to bring the lost to the safe and abundant harbor that is redemption in Christ. A clean, passionate heart for Christ will give us unhindered prayer power. The Holy Spirit uses this power to seek, save, and transform the lost.

Prayer—Ask the Lord to reveal any area of your life where you have not made Him Lord. Recognize that this area in your life hinders your prayers for the lost. Place your seekers' prayer requests in God's hands.

Care—Demonstrate your care for those on your prayer list by your own holy, righteous, and godly life. Be a builder of faith in others by praying for them.

Share—Share with your accountability prayer partner one personal disappointment in your life that you can turn into a witnessing illustration "appointment." Share a confession of anything that has hindered your prayer life.

Sail on Over to Day 6—Complete questions 10-12 of the review summary for day 6.

Charting My Course on Day 7—Based on today's reading, alter or add to your plan of action by charting your course on day 7.

Thought for the Day—Prayer is not me motivating God to save my family member or friend; it is me being motivated to do my part.

DAY 5

Challenge Question—Where are those on my prayer list?
Reread—John 17:15-19

Jesus said, "Peace be with you! As the Father has sent me, I am sending you" (John 20:21). Does that sound like an obligation to you? Sometimes with our fast-paced, busy schedules the last thing we want to hear is another obligation. Yet there is an obligation that is light, positive, uplifting, and regenerating. It demands our utmost attention. We have an obligation to exhibit the peace that passes all understanding to those around us, whether saved or unsaved. Peace is a gift of eternal life—the very meaning of Christmas.

All week you have been examining spiritual preparations to equip you for sharing. In order to radiate as a Lighthouse you must imitate Jesus—being spiritually clean, boldly confident, supported by holy intercessors, empowered with holy passion, and persevering in faith. That is a big order! But with God all things are possible. With Jesus as your Intercessor, God will use your accountability partner to encourage and challenge you to become all that He intended. It is the devil himself who has been trying to divert you from the biggest blessing in your spiritual journey—sharing God's plan of love and peace with others. Those on your prayer list are just one step closer to knowing and obeying Christ because of your commitment to godly prayer, caring, and sharing this week. Don't let anyone or anything steal your joy in radiating the love of Jesus.

Prayer—Ask God to help you demonstrate His peace, love, and joy to all those around you, especially to those on your prayer list. Ask God to move powerfully in the lives of your seekers to make His joy known.

Care—Implement one idea from the Care List for each seeker on your prayer list.

Share—Ask those on your prayer list if they see peace, love, and joy in your life. Listen closely to their responses in how they see differences in you.

Sail on Over to Day 6—Complete questions 13-15 of the review summary for day 6.

Charting My Course on Day 7—Based on today's reading, alter or add to your plan of action by charting your course on day 7.

Thought for the Day—With Jesus as your Intercessor, God will use your accountability partner to encourage and challenge you to become all that He intended.

DAY 6

Review Summary

Questions 1-15

1. What is our incentive to pray for the lost?

2. Why is prayer the first step in witnessing?

3. What does "fervent" prayer mean to you?

4. Why does the prompting from the Holy Spirit precede witnessing?

5. What do you think the Bible means by the peace that passes all understanding (Phil. 4:7)?

6. Why do the people on your prayer list need this understanding?

7. Why is it important for disciples to be obedient as well as saved?

8. Who is on your winning witnessing team?

9. How is your accountability partner a strong team member?

10. Who and what seeks to hinder our prayers?

11. Who helps us withstand persecution?

12. Why is a holy life important to our witness?

14. What makes a radiant Lighthouse?

13. What obligations do you have that are a joy to you?

15. Who would want to steal your Lighthouse joy this next week?

DAY 7

Charting My Course

Based on this week's readings, alter or add to your plan of action by charting your course.

	Name	Prayer Action	Care Action	Share Action	Prayer Answer
Day 1					
Day 2					
Day 3					
Day 4					
Day 5					
Day 6					
Day 7					

Week 3—A Winning Lighthouse

DAY 1

Challenge Question—What should I pray for lost people?

Read—John 8:12

Specific prayers glean specific answers. In praying for the unsaved we must pray for several specific things. First, we are to pray that God would draw the unsaved to himself (John 6:44). Jesus is the Lighthouse, and we are His rays of light. Just as a beacon of light shining from a lighthouse draws ships to a safe harbor, God sometimes guides people to salvation with the spiritual light they see in your life.

We are also to pray that the lost will seek to know God. Sometimes we think our lost family members or friends are not seeking after the things of God. When praying for them to thirst after God, pray for them by name that they will seek Him and not their own ways.

Although the Bible is the complete, infallible, inspired foundation for each moment of our life, only God can compel the heart to accept this fact. Satan will try to blind people from the truth of Scripture. Just as people often wear blindfolds to avoid light while sleeping, the devil tries to blind the unsaved to God's light by encouraging them to do evil. Pray that God will remove the blinders from their souls.

When our loved ones are in the hospital we visit them to show our love and care. In the same way we must pray for unbelievers out of love for them and ask the Holy Spirit to visit them in a personal way to guide them to truth (John 16:8-13). If it is not us that God intends to use to bring those we love to salvation, we must pray that He will send *someone* (Matt. 9:37-38).

Witnessing is a team effort. Some sow, some water, some reap. Sometimes we may witness to a friend for years and then a stranger may say a word that immediately makes the gospel real. Thank God for the many ways He uses our Christian brothers and sisters to win the lost.

Prayer—Petition God in each of the scriptural prayer areas for each name on your prayer list.

Care—Introduce yourself to other Christians who are acquainted with those on your prayer list and offer to support them in witnessing to your friend.

Share—Share the needs of those on your prayer list with your prayer partner this week.

Sail on Over to Day 6—Complete questions 1-3 of the review summary for day 6.

Charting My Course on Day 7—Based on today's reading, alter or add to your plan of action by charting your course on day 7.

Thought for the Day—Just as a beacon of light shining from a lighthouse draws ships to a safe harbor, God sometimes guides people to salvation with the spiritual light they see in your life.

DAY 2

Challenge Question—Why are specific prayers for the lost important?

Reread—John 8:12

Action Item—Define the term *spiritual darkness.*

A seeker often does not realize he or she is in spiritual darkness. Morals in our society are blurred and vague. Lying is an accepted norm. One in three people is abused. Violence is glamorized in various ways. Marriage is in question as a firm standard. Business ethics are deferred for bottom-line profits. Political correctness is heralded as a model of morality. Most people do not even know what sin is.

We must define the biblical standard of morality in everyday life. We must help the lost realize that repentance without permanent turning from sin is not enough. They must feel so sorry for wrongdoing that they desire never to turn from God again. We must help the unsaved foster genuine sorrow for wrongdoing by bringing it to their attention lovingly, directly, and uncompromisingly (Acts 3:19).

John 1:12 says, "Yet to all who received him, to those who believed in his name, he gave the right to become children of God." The key word in this verse is "received," which means the person has believed *and* accepted. We must pray the unsaved will *believe.* The Lordship of Christ is the most misunderstood of salvation principles. Many have never understood that Jesus must come first, before family, work, good deeds, everything. Specifically pray for your loved ones to know Jesus as Savior and Lord.

Prayer—Ask God to help you defend where, when, and why biblical moral standards are still important in practical everyday circumstances. Bring your seekers' requests to God.

Care—Invite those on your prayer list to your home to see your wholesome family up close and personal. The difference between your Christian family and other families should be obvious.

Share—Clearly explain to others this week the importance of biblical standards in a circumstance God brings your way.

Sail on Over to Day 6—Complete questions 4-6 of the review summary for day 6.

Charting My Course on Day 7—Based on today's reading, alter or add to your plan of action by charting your course on day 7.

Thought for the Day—The Lordship of Christ is the most misunderstood of the salvation principles. Jesus comes first before family, work, or good deeds.

DAY 3

Challenge Question—What makes me an authority?
Read—John 8:12
Action Item—Define what it is that makes one *authoritative*.

While our society offers up many experts on how to lead our lives, we know that all of these without God will fall short. Good deeds cannot save our souls. Religion cannot save our souls. Being good people cannot save our souls. So what makes Christians authorities on how to live? They have had real experiences with Jesus and so have learned that all other ways of living never bring the peace we seek. Witnessing is simply sharing with others what we have experienced.

We must pray for new or growing Christians to become grounded in biblical truth—the final, authoritative Word of God. We do not have to be concerned with making righteous judgments in determining someone else's spiritual state. Look at Engel's Evangelistic Countdown (Appendix H) to see the many steps it takes to move toward spiritual maturity. We must pray that both the lost and new Christians grow in Christ. We are only accountable to encourage them to continue taking one step closer to God than they were before. God is the final Judge of our spiritual maturity in relation to himself. We cannot be authorities over what is God's responsibility, but we can be authorities in bringing the message of truth to others.

Prayer—Ask God to help you determine where each of your seekers is on Engel's Evangelistic Countdown, and ask Him to use you to help them move one step closer to following Him.

Care—Choose one of your own Care List ideas and implement it.

Share—Practice sharing with your accountability partner how you have personally moved through Engel's Evangelistic Countdown so you are at ease in sharing your experience.

Sail on Over to Day 6—Complete questions 7-9 of the review summary for day 6.

Charting My Course on Day 7—Based on today's reading, alter or add to your plan of action by charting your course on day 7.

Thought for the Day—Witnessing is simply sharing with others what we have experienced.

DAY 4

Challenge Question—Who wins the lost?
Action Item—Memorize John 8:12.

The Holy Spirit draws, reveals, convicts, confirms, compels, and personalizes God the Father and Son to humanity. The Holy Spirit resides in the hearts and lives of believers. Asking people how we can pray for them is an effective witnessing technique. The Holy Spirit uses our questions to convict those hearts gone astray. If we don't follow the prompting of the Holy Spirit in our lives, how will the lost see God's work in us?

Sin can be both categorical and uniquely individual. There are sins that everyone is tempted by, such as envy, greed, and jealousy. There are also sins specific to some individuals: alcoholism, sexual addiction, and gluttony. It has been said that God does not care so much about specific sins as He does about the rebellion that causes them. John Wesley once asked his mother what sin was. She replied, "Whatever weakens your sense of reason, impairs the tenderness of your conscience, obscures your sense of God, or takes off the relish of spiritual things . . . that thing is sin to you."

Only the Holy Spirit can make us fully aware of times when God is speaking. Matt. 9:38 reminds us to "ask the Lord of the harvest . . . to send out workers into his harvest field." God is always prompting harvesters, not observers. The fields are white unto harvest; we need to heed the Holy Spirit's prompting to share God's love. The fact is, there are billions of people who are beyond our personal reach. They may be mentally, physically, or emotionally beyond our scope. However, when the Holy Spirit comes upon us, we will be bold witnesses through whom the Spirit attracts seekers to God. Our prayers are effective in winning to Christ those outside our spheres of influence. We must be God's conduits of love wherever He has placed us and assist those we *are* able to reach. Leave the rest to God.

Prayer—Express to God your desire to be open to the prompting of the Holy Spirit, and confess any of the times when you may have quenched the Spirit. Thank God for hearing your prayer requests on behalf of those on your prayer list.

Care—Give affirming comments or hugs to your seekers this week.

Share—Ask your unsaved friends for specific prayer requests and help them form the requests in a biblically sound manner. For example, reform a prayer request for lottery winning to a request for having their spiritual needs supplied. Be gentle and instructive.

Sail on Over to Day 6—Complete questions 10-12 of the review summary for day 6.

Charting My Course on Day 7—Based on today's reading, alter or add to your plan of action by charting your course on day 7.

Thought for the Day—If we don't follow the prompting of the Holy Spirit in our lives, how will the lost see God's work in us?

DAY 5

Challenge Question—Where are those on your Prayer, Care, Share lists now?

Action Item—Recite from memory John 8:12.

As you have been faithfully praying for the three to five people God has placed on your heart, you may have had opportunities to witness to them in big and small ways. By now you have been giving God your nervousness for three weeks. Only the power of the Holy Spirit can take away your nervousness. Prior to my cousin receiving an award from the queen of England for outstanding service, she was given instruction on how to curtsy, how to address the queen, and how she should not feel nervous if she forgot something. You may feel the same nervousness when witnessing about the King of all Kings. That is OK; just don't stop sharing the gospel for any reason. Those on your prayer list know where you stand now, even if they have not yet accepted Christ.

Those you are witnessing to may be exhibiting signs that show they are becoming aware of the gospel message. You may be noticing less profanity from them. You may notice their enthusiasm to impress you with good deeds. They may attend church as a sign of their progress. Remember that all things God allows in your life can be used for the good of those on your prayer list. They need to see you going through all the same things they do, but with the help of prayer. Even a stay in the hospital can win to Christ someone who sees you live out your faith through difficult circumstances. Although you are still human, you're redeemed by God's grace. Be transparent in your frailties and liberal with the reason for your faith.

Prayer—Ask God to remove any nervousness or discomfort you may still have when sharing your faith. Confess any witnessing opportunities you may have missed by considering your own nervousness.

Care—Now would be a good time to drop a Christian greeting card to each of those on your prayer list, mentioning specifically that you are praying for them.

Share—Find a way to affirm the spiritual progress you are observing in the people for whom you are praying. They will be glad you noticed and will be encouraged to continue their spiritual growth.

Sail on Over to Day 6—Complete questions 13-15 of the review summary for day 6.

Charting My Course on Day 7—Based on today's reading, alter or add to your plan of action by charting your course on day 7.

Thought for the Day—Be transparent in your frailties and liberal with the reason for your faith.

DAY 6

Review Summary

Questions 1-15

1. Why are specific prayers effective?

2. How can God move to bring His truth into focus for the unsaved?

3. In what ways are you sowing and watering in the lives of those on your prayer list?

4. Why is repentance without permanent turning from sin not enough for salvation?

5. What moral standards are those in your sphere of influence violating?

6. How can we gain faith that overcomes the fear of sharing the gospel?

7. In what ways are those on your prayer list trying to rationalize their way to heaven?

8. How can believers be spiritual authorities?

9. Where are the people on your prayer list on Engel's Evangelistic Countdown?

10. Who wins the lost to Jesus Christ?

11. Who convicts the sinner of sin?

12. How can we quench the Holy Spirit?

13. What should we do with our feelings of nervousness?

14. What changes in lifestyle or attitudes are you noticing in your lost friends?

15. How can you bring good out of a difficult circumstance or conversation?

DAY 7

Charting My Course

Based on this week's readings, alter or add to your plan of action by charting your course.

	Name	Prayer Action	Care Action	Share Action	Prayer Answer
Day 1					
Day 2					
Day 3					
Day 4					
Day 5					
Day 6					
Day 7					

Week 4—A Persevering Lighthouse

DAY 1

Challenge Question—How often should I pray?

Read—1 Thess. 5:17

Action Item—Define the phrase *without ceasing.*

Praying, asking, and believing are integral daily activities for believers. Matt. 26:41 reminds us to "watch and pray." The Lord will reveal to us just how to pray for others if we ask. We will not stop praying for someone we care about. We are to be devoted to prayer with an attitude of thanksgiving and should expect God to open doors for us to present the gospel clearly. When your prayers do not seem to be working, take heart. We "should always pray and not give up" (Luke 18:1). I have been praying for some of my family for over 20 years to know Christ personally and still I continue to pray for them.

George Mueller once said, "The point is . . . never give up until the answer comes." To pray without ceasing for the unsaved means we must daily intercede on their behalf, invest prayerfully in acts of kindness and love, invite them to God-honoring events, implore them to respond to the gospel, and imagine them as His followers. God will move them closer to Him with your focused, specific, and ongoing prayer.

Prayer—Ask God to reveal to you what it means for your life to "pray continually" (1 Thess. 5:17). Continue to petition God on behalf of your seekers' needs.

Care—Make a "walk date" with those on your prayer list, and use the opportunity to discuss their spiritual walk.

Share—Follow up on the prayer requests from each person on your prayer list. Commit to continuing in prayer on their behalf. Share with those on your list how privileged you are to pray for them.

Sail on Over to Day 6—Complete questions 1-3 of the review summary for day 6.

Charting My Course on Day 7—Based on today's reading, alter or add to your plan of action by charting your course on day 7.

Thought for the Day—We are to be devoted to prayer with an attitude of thanksgiving.

DAY 2

Challenge Question—How should I go about praying daily for the lost?

Read—1 Thess. 5:16-18

Action Item—Name the three main verbs in the text for today.

Those around us observe our behavior and conduct but only God sees our conduct in prayer. How we enter into His holy presence is a personal matter. However, I have found the acrostic ACTS helpful in prayer approach: A for "Adoration of who God is," C for "Confession of any intentional or unintentional sin in my life," T for the "Thanksgiving of what God has done in my life and those around me," and S for "Supplication," meaning petitioning through prayer for others as well as yourself. We are reminded in 1 Thess. 5:16-18 to approach God in a rejoicing, prayerful, and thankful attitude.

As a Christian you may be led to fast and pray for your seekers. Our humble, joyful, trusting, and hopeful attitudes in prayer will produce powerful agreement between us and God. Prayer changes us and others. Our minds and spirits are renewed in prayer so that as we face another day we can approach it with confidence knowing that the God of the universe is walking with us. Therefore, we must be vigilant and keep our spiritual walls strong.

This is especially important when we witness to people. Witnessing is the front line in the spiritual battle. It is our choice to put on our spiritual armor for the battle. Prayer before the day begins protects us. Having a continual attitude of prayer keeps our minds and hearts dwelling on the things of God. Public prayers acknowledge our priorities before God and others. Family altar prayers instruct our families, unite our homes as His sanctuaries, and bring blessings on our residences as a safe harbor for the lost. Go about prayer reverently and often.

Prayer—Ask God to help you strengthen your prayer life. Confess any area of your prayer life that is not pleasing to Him. Ask Him to protect your daily devotions by helping you be disciplined in your consistency.

Care—Write out one of the prayer requests someone on your list has made. Send it to that person as a way of showing you are still remembering him or her in prayer.

Share—Share with those on your prayer list specifically how God is leading you to pray. As the answers to these prayers unfold they will see God as the Author of their faith.

Sail on Over to Day 6—Complete questions 4-6 of the review summary for day 6.

Charting My Course on Day 7—Based on today's reading, alter or add to your plan of action by charting your course on day 7.

Thought for the Day—Prayer changes us and others.

DAY 3

Challenge Question—How are my prayers working?

Review—1 Thess. 5:17

Action Item—Highlight key words in the text for today.

In 1 Corinthians the apostle Paul reminds us that the god of this world has blinded the minds of the unbelieving, so that they would not see the glorious gospel of Christ.

As you pray for the blinders to come off the eyes of the lost you will see a greater thirst and hunger for God developing in their lives. Those you pray for may be mentioning prayer, God, church, or some spiritual reference in their conversations with you. These are signs that your prayers are working and that they are coming closer to God.

While we are praying for those blinders to come off, we need to be gently correcting them if they are still in opposition to the things of God. Our gentle correction should encourage them in escaping the devil's hold and accepting the forgiveness offered to a repentant heart. Only God can "set the captives free," but you can show them the key to their prison door. Remember the eyes and ears of the lost have become dull to the things of God. Their hearts have become hardened without understanding. Pray for them to return to the God of their creation and accept His healing.

You may begin to notice how God has sent other Christians into the lives of your seekers to confirm His truth and His providential touch on their lives. Continue to pray for the Lord to send more witnessing teammates to work alongside you. Remember, "Devote yourselves to prayer, keeping alert in it with an attitude of thanksgiving, praying at the same time . . . that God will open to [you] a door for the word, so that [you] may speak forth the mystery of Christ" (Col. 4:2-3, NASB).

Prayer—Ask God to create a spiritual hunger, remove the blinders, and give the lost ears to hear, faith to believe, and the will to respond to His saving love.

Care—Select a care idea from your Care List to implement this week.

Share—Ask those on your prayer list how they have seen answers to your prayers for them.

Sail on Over to Day 6—Complete questions 7-9 of the review summary for day 6.

Charting My Course on Day 7—Based on today's reading, alter or add to your plan of action by charting your course on day 7.

Thought for the Day—The eyes and ears of the lost have become dull to the things of God. Their hearts have become hardened without understanding.

DAY 4

Challenge Question—How do I pray for family members?
Memorize—1 Thess. 5:17
Action Item—Quote 1 Thess. 5:17 during family devotions.

Praying for boldness to witness is vital, especially when it comes to witnessing to family members with whom you are emotionally attached. You may feel bound with the fear of rejection or isolation if you share Christ boldly. Holidays may be especially difficult with unsaved family members, yet when you pray ask God to keep your emotions from getting in the way of gently, sensitively sharing your faith.

Whenever you take a stand based on your Christian values, you *may* feel some discomfort. Prayerfully keeping a vision of your loved ones at peace with God will help keep you from compromising. God will bless your obedience and give you confidence as you continue to witness (Acts 4:29). Sometimes we think Jesus can take away the sins of the whole world but not those of our family members. God may use someone or something else to witness to your family. You must keep praying no matter how long it takes.

Prayer—Ask God to give you boldness to witness by both your words and your lifestyle. Ask Him to give you boldness to witness to those with whom it may be more difficult or require greater risk or sacrifice. Ask Him to keep the vision in front of you of your loved ones at peace with Him.

Care—During Advent or Easter take a short story, devotional, or hymn with you to your family reunion to reinforce the meaning of the holidays.

Share—Share one thing for which you are thankful to God about your family. Tell each one personally or with a special note what you are thankful for about him or her.

Sail on Over to Day 6—Complete questions 10-12 of the review summary for day 6.

Charting My Course on Day 7—Based on today's reading, alter or add to your plan of action by charting your course on day 7.

Thought for the Day—Prayerfully keeping a vision of your loved ones at peace with God will help keep you from compromising.

DAY 5

Challenge Question—Where are those on your prayer list now?

Action Item—Recite 1 Thess. 5:17.

Praying for the lost to come to Christ sometimes requires long hours and great diligence. We are to be models of prayer to unbelievers. They should readily know they can come to us for prayer. Asking you to pray for them should become quite natural. They should feel comfortable with your *confidentiality* and demonstrate trust in your prayers.

In the Book of James, Elijah is held up as a model of prayer. He prayed for a drought and even his own water supply dried up! His prayers were inconvenient and uncomfortable for him personally but had a defined purpose—the salvation of others to glorify God. Those on your prayer list must also feel that you will pray for them even if it may be inconvenient or uncomfortable for you. They may ask you to pray for them out loud. People are often moved to tears when hearing their name and request in a public conversational prayer. Strangers in physical proximity to you (such as people in a restaurant or hospital bed) may feel the Spirit's touch when they overhear you pray. Thankfulness for your daily bread may be your best witness.

Mother Teresa was a model of prayer to those around her. She made complete silence a part of her daily prayer vigil to help her focus on her Master completely. The next time you toss and turn on a sleepless night, try using the time wisely by petitioning God on behalf of the unsaved on your prayer list. Remember, if you will intercede, invest, invite, implore, and imagine without ceasing for those on your Lighthouse prayer list, God will move them closer to himself.

Prayer—Confess any time you neglected to pray for someone because it was inconvenient or time-consuming. Ask God to make you a model of prayer. Thank Him for answering prayer on behalf of those on your prayer list.

Care—Select a care idea from your Care List and implement it this week.

Share—Relate to those on your list one area where God is helping you grow. It may even be in the area of discipline in prayer. Be sure to remain honest and open.

Sail on Over to Day 6—Complete questions 13-15 of the review summary for day 6.

Charting My Course on Day 7—Based on today's reading, alter or add to your plan of action by charting your course on day 7.

Thought for the Day—Thankfulness for your daily bread may be your best witness.

DAY 6

Review Summary

Questions 1-15

1. What does "pray continually" mean to you?

2. How often should we pray?

3. What do fervent and unceasing prayers have in common?

4. How do you approach God in prayer each day?

5. Why is our prayer attitude important?

6. Who wants to distract, steal, divert, and destroy our prayer time? What can we do about it?

7. What signs are you seeing that your seekers are coming closer to God?

8. How are their hearts being softened toward spiritual things?

9. Who or what has God allowed in their lives to nudge them forward?

10. Why is prayer for family members so important?

11. What has God promised He will do to help? (See Acts 4:29.)

12. What does pleading to God for our loved ones mean?

13. How are you being a model of prayer to those around you?

14. What is a conversational prayer and how can it be effective?

15. What are the five things we can do to move people closer to God?

DAY 7

Charting My Course

Based on this week's readings, alter or add to your plan of action by charting your course.

	Name	Prayer Action	Care Action	Share Action	Prayer Answer
Day 1					
Day 2					
Day 3					
Day 4					
Day 5					
Day 6					
Day 7					

Week 5—A Caring Lighthouse

DAY 1

Challenge Question—Why is care important?

Read—Mark 12:30-31

Action Item—Name the two greatest commandments.

Dr. John Maxwell said, "People don't care how much you know until they know how much you care." In order to love God with all of our heart, soul, mind, and strength we must also demonstrate the second commandment to love our neighbor as ourselves. Dare to make a difference by showing simple acts of kindness. Love expressed in tangible ways speaks volumes to those around you. The simple gifts of hospitality and service can meet the deepest needs of the heart.

Jesus met strategic needs in order to soften the hearts of people for the things of God. He was a servant-leader in the truest sense. The ancient Jews were convinced that keeping the first and second commandments was their spiritual aim in life. These commandments are at the soul of the gospel. Did Jesus meet every need? No, He was Father-centered and redemptive in all that He did. He responded to the needs of people as the Holy Spirit prompted Him. We, too, must respond to the needs of others out of a grateful heart toward God, for all that He has done and is doing in our lives. Love should be our motivation. In a way, meeting the genuine needs of others is like singing a song of thanks to our Lord. It brings us personal satisfaction to know we are pleasing Him. Just as Christ was proud of the widow who gave all she had to live on (Mark 12:43-44), God cares more about our obedience than our acts.

It could be said that the world has a kindness deficit. As Christians, we can make a powerful difference in the lives of others when we demonstrate sincere concern for them. That is why the Scriptures say it is more blessed to give than to receive. When we give out of love for God, we receive the greatest blessing.

Prayer—Ask God to prompt you to acts of kindness that will soften the hearts of the lost. Bring any new seekers' prayer requests to God.

Care—As God prompts you, meet a need for those on your prayer list. It may be just a note or call. Let those on your prayer list know you are thinking of them this week by calling them or sending them a short note.

Share—Each time you exhibit an act of kindness that others notice, make sure you give God the credit for prompting you. Be a name-dropper for God.

Sail on Over to Day 6—Complete questions 1-3 of the review summary for day 6.

Charting My Course on Day 7—Based on today's reading, alter or add to your plan of action by charting your course on day 7.

Thought for the Day—When we give out of love for God, we receive the greatest blessing.

DAY 2

Challenge Question—Who should show care for the lost?
Reread—Mark 12:30-31

When we love others into a saving knowledge of God, we may get all "messy" involving ourselves in their lives. But even Jesus was a friend of sinners despite their messy lives. We are to be in the world, loving and caring for the lost, but not of it, participating in their sin. If we do not care for those around us, who will? Before we came to know Christ and began to follow Him, we did not really know how to love. Now we do. And now we must.

A recent Gallup poll revealed that many people rank friendship among their greatest needs. What a friend we have in Jesus! Thankfully Jesus also teaches us how to be a true friend. He is always available, dependable, and responsible. We can tell Him anything and He understands. For the unsaved, we can be a friend who stays when others walk out. We can be there for our seekers when others let them down or are against them. They will never forget our love during the hard times.

It has been said, "A good friend laughs with you and doubles the laughter; and cries with you, and cuts the pain in half." Times of stress and pain are good witnessing opportunities—funerals, illness, divorce, job loss—are all times in life when the world offers no hope or encouragement. We, however, serve a God who will never let us down. After the Day of Pentecost many miraculous conversions took place because believers responded to the needy and gave them what they had. We must let the lost know that all we own belongs to God and that we will care for them.

Prayer—Ask God to help keep you from pulling away from the messy lives of the unsaved and to help you enter in where others fear to tread. Ask God to help you discover a daring act of kindness that will soften the hearts of your seekers toward Him.

Care—Dare to demonstrate the love of God by an act or gesture of kindness that others would find impossible. It will speak volumes of God's love.

Share—Remind the recipient with your caring acts that Jesus is the One who causes you to know their needs and have the strength to respond to them.

Sail on Over to Day 6—Complete questions 4-6 of the review summary for day 6.

Charting My Course on Day 7—Based on today's reading, alter or add to your plan of action by charting your course on day 7.

Thought for the Day—A good friend laughs with you and doubles the laughter; and cries with you, and cuts the pain in half.

DAY 3

Challenge Question—What happens when I care?
Action Item—Memorize Mark 12:31.

When we ask God to help us find ways to build caring relationships with nonbelievers, He will open the doors for us to share the gospel. If we ask God for specific ways to demonstrate care beyond the recipients' expectations and then act on the ideas He gives us, and the seekers will be more open to listen to the gospel. That is why we sing the chorus "They Will Know We Are Christians by Our Love."

Our relationships with others are the testing grounds of our faith. When we share the gospel, people will only respond to the depth of our level of care for them. Jesus becomes real to them when we respond to their felt needs. If we extend grace, they will understand grace. If we extend forgiveness, they will understand forgiveness. No matter how you ask an unsaved person, "Do you want to be a Christian?" what they hear is, "Do you want to be like me?" We should make it our business to help others feel comfortable in our presence while still holding firmly to our convictions.

Remember the scripture in John 21 referring to feeding lambs and caring for sheep? Notice that "caring" comes before "sharing" Christ and leading others to follow Him. Tending actual lambs is a vigilant process. Lambs would die but for a shepherd methodically guarding, guiding, sheltering, and feeding them. Our job is to assist the Shepherd in seeking and caring for the lambs He places in our path. Lambs can easily become frightened, directionless, and unclean. Our self-sufficient world would lure us into neglecting the needs of others. But our Savior said that if we love Him we will tend to the needs of the lost.

Prayer—Ask God to show you how the love He has given you can help bring others to Christ. He may show you a frailty turned for God's good. Continue praying for your seeker requests.

Care—Choose a Care List idea that fits the current needs for those on your prayer list.

Share—Share how your friend Jesus shows grace and forgiveness to you and how He wants to extend it to the lost as well.

Sail on Over to Day 6—Complete questions 7-9 of the review summary for day 6.

Charting My Course on Day 7—Based on today's reading, alter or add to your plan of action by charting your course on day 7.

Thought for the Day—No matter how you ask an unsaved person, "Do you want to be a Christian?" what they hear is, "Do you want to be like me?"

DAY 4

Challenge Question—Where can I show care?
Action Item—Recite Mark 12:31.

People will hear and see the hope of salvation when they know we genuinely care for their deepest needs. If a seeker's deepest need is self-esteem, find ways to encourage that person. If it is a physical need, find a way to support him or her tangibly. If it is social, introduce your seekers to your friends. Only when people experience the love of God will they be forever changed.

Being faithful in the little things demonstrates your care. That Scripture verse on your kitchen wall, the verse at the end of a greeting card, a telephone message after a difficult day—they all add up to say you care. Sometimes we wonder if taking that extra hour on the way home from work to make a hospital visit makes a difference. All of these gestures tell others that Jesus lives in our hearts and priorities. Be faithful in the little things, for in due time they will reap the reward of salvation in the heart of a friend.

When we care deeply about others, we will want to give them the very best of our time, talents, and gifts—not the remnants of our time. You may have to sacrifice the privacy of having Thanksgiving with your family alone to include nonbelievers. But when you pray and share what you are thankful for, it will surely soften their hearts for God and cure the pangs of isolation they feel during the holidays. There are ways to show you care everywhere there is a need.

Prayer—Ask God to reveal to you the deepest needs within the hearts of those on your prayer list. Ask Him to show you how you can respond to these needs to demonstrate His love.

Care—Invite a nonbeliever to your home during a particularly lonely time for him or her.

Share—Share with a nonbeliever what you are thankful for. When he or she asks what makes you so different, say that God has filled your life with a love beyond yourself.

Sail on Over to Day 6—Complete questions 10-12 of the review summary for day 6.

Charting My Course on Day 7—Based on today's reading, alter or add to your plan of action by charting your course on day 7.

Thought for the Day—"How beautiful are the feet of those who bring good news!" (Rom. 10:15).

DAY 5

Challenge Question—Where are those on your prayer list now?

Read—Mark 12:31

Action Item—Determine who your neighbor is.

The apostle Paul, in 1 Thess. 5:14, says: "Admonish the unruly, encourage the fainthearted, help the weak, be patient with everyone" (NASB). Any parent knows that disciplining children is a hard but important aspect to good parenting. Setting limits makes children feel secure and loved and brings long-term obedience to God. In the same sense we must lovingly admonish unbelievers as God opens the door of salvation. Often they do not know they are going astray.

By now you may have had to instruct your friend in some biblical standard that made him or her feel uncomfortable or under conviction. Straying from God occurs when seekers think good works, religion, philosophy, or morality will save them. They are eternally separated from God and may not even know it. It is important to set boundaries in your relationships with them, or they will never understand God has set boundaries for their own good. Clear boundaries foster trust, security, love, good moral standards, and obedience to God. Gentle and consistent, loving admonishment will alert seekers to how they have gone astray.

Prayer—Ask God to help you be patient with your unsaved friends. Bring your seekers' prayer requests to Him today.

Care—Care enough to set behavioral limits on the unsaved. No one else has.

Share—Share how God loves us so much that He has given us a plan for our lives in order to enjoy abundant life. God has set boundaries because He loves us.

Sail on Over to Day 6—Complete questions 13-15 of the review summary for day 6.

Charting My Course on Day 7—Based on today's reading, alter or add to your plan of action by charting your course on day 7.

Thought for the Day—Clear boundaries foster trust, security, love, good moral standards, and obedience to God.

DAY 6

Review Summary

Questions 1-15

1. Why is genuine care for others important?

2. Who needs a caring gesture from you today?

3. What makes compassionate caring so effective in witnessing?

4. Why do people need friendship so much today?

5. Why are the stressful times of life good witnessing opportunities?

6. What does it take to react like a true Christian?

7. What are some ways you can tend the lost who God has entrusted to your care?

8. Can you explain grace and forgiveness?

9. Why is consistent caring so powerful?

10. Identify the deepest needs of those on your prayer list.

11. Why is being faithful in the little things so powerful?

12. What important moments in the lives of others have you been a part of to show you care? How did this bring someone closer to Christ?

13. When do you overlook unruliness and when do you correctively instruct?

15. Where have you shown patience beyond yourself to the unsaved?

14. What does "you were like sheep going astray" (1 Pet. 2:25) mean?

DAY 7

Charting My Course

Based on this week's readings, alter or add to your plan of action by charting your course.

	Name	Prayer Action	Care Action	Share Action	Prayer Answer
Day 1					
Day 2					
Day 3					
Day 4					
Day 5					
Day 6					
Day 7					

Week 6—A Securing Lighthouse

DAY 1

Challenge Question—How does my life make others feel safe to share?

Read—Ps. 142:4

Just as a Lighthouse beacons a ship to safe harbor, your Christian home must represent a safe, loving harbor for the lost you have been praying for. Think about it—you have modeled Jesus to the unbeliever, but have you also modeled God as safe and trustworthy for your own children? The multiplication of your labors is eternal. Providing security is a much-needed element of care in which the world has failed miserably.

Despite decades of awareness, starvation is still common in much of the world and government programs have not been able to defeat poverty. Prov. 29:7 reminds us that "the righteous care about justice for the poor, but the wicked have no such concern." As believers we know the only answer for the deep social and economic impoverishment within our world is a transformation that only Jesus can bring. Food without the Giver of food falls short. When He lived on earth Jesus was so attractive to follow because He befriended sinners, Gentiles, women, and people of all backgrounds. He defied the social boundaries of His day to bring an eternal message. We have similar boundaries today: racial, denominational, religious, political, and cultural. We need to be courageous, strong believers who are not afraid to cross these temporal boundaries to bring the boundary-shattering Good News to all people. Jesus can be the common denominator to bring true peace to our world. Our lives must bring a sense of the security that only God offers. Jesus builds up all people. He sees them with divine eyes and knows what they can become. People feel free to open up and be transparent to Him. He helps them find the eternal, secure life they desire. We must do likewise by holding confidences, being loyal, and being trustworthy. Then we must share with them the only One worthy of our trust.

Prayer—Ask God to help you become a safe harbor for the unsaved. Pray for the prayer requests your seekers have entrusted to you.

Care—Select a care idea that will help your unsaved friends feel secure and know you care about them.

Share—Share with those on your unsaved prayer list how Jesus is the only One who can fulfill their deep needs for security and lasting peace.

Sail on Over to Day 6—Complete questions 1-3 of the review summary for day 6.

Charting My Course on Day 7—Based on today's reading, alter or add to your plan of action by charting your course on day 7.

Thought for the Day—Our lives must bring to others a sense of the security that only God offers.

DAY 2

Challenge Question—How can I build secure, caring relationships?

Read—Ps. 142:4

Have you ever met someone who seems to bring out the best in others? People like that are a joy to be around. They make you feel good about yourself and that you are important. Jesus' disciples learned to also become all things to all men, so that some would be saved (1 Cor. 9:22).

Jesus modeled the effectiveness of treating people differently depending on their needs. He knew whether they needed acts of service, kind words, or affectionate understanding. He offered that which He knew would move their hearts. Christ loved the unlovely, always seeing what they could become, not what they were without Him. He knew how to encourage them on their spiritual journeys. For example, He understood Nicodemus was a religious man who had no knowledge of being born again. He knew the heart of the woman who lavishly poured oil on His feet. He respected everyone and placed value on each person.

Finding likable traits in people can be a challenge sometimes, yet when we encourage them in their strengths it helps them confront their shortcomings. Encouragement helps people feel secure enough to open up to us despite feeling vulnerable. Then they will learn to make themselves vulnerable to God. Remember secure, caring friendships are only earned over time.

Prayer—Pray for God to help you bring out the best in others. Ask Him to show you what actions your seekers will understand best.

Care—Take time to humbly serve one of your seekers in a way that will amaze him or her for God.

Share—Share with your seekers that it is Jesus who teaches you how to be the kind of friend who is rare in today's culture.

Sail on Over to Day 6—Complete questions 4-6 of the review summary for day 6.

Charting My Course on Day 7—Based on today's reading, alter or add to your plan of action by charting your course on day 7.

Thought for the Day—Christ loved the unlovely, always seeing what they could become, not what they were without Him.

DAY 3

Challenge Question—Am I modeling the love of Jesus?

Recite—Ps. 142:4

Action Item—Define the term *respect*.

According to Rom. 3:23, we have all fallen short of God's glory, but He still loves us. If there was ever someone who had a right to be arrogant, it was Jesus, yet He showed what it was to be humble. He washed the feet of His disciples, modeling humility and servanthood. As Christians we must be careful not to flaunt our privileged position as children of God. We should, however, seek ways to lift others up in order that they, too, will join us in the abundant life. Washing the dishes after a friend's party, preparing a meal for a single mom, or shoveling snow for a neighbor are all humble acts that can show God's love.

Sometimes you may feel bombarded by language and lifestyle choices that are different from yours. And it may take months or years to cultivate some relationships where there is dramatic cultural diversity. But we are called to be salt and light wherever we are. How we treat a beautician who has just given us a "bad hair day" may open the door for a presentation of the gospel. Some people will feel like they can share anything with you, because you demonstrate compassion, understanding, and encouragement on a consistent basis.

Always look for ways to encourage seekers. When they see your godly walk and hear your godly talk, they will feel safe enough to share their deepest needs for God. You may be the only Jesus they will ever know.

Prayer—Thank God that He still loves you when you mess up. Ask Him to help you be patient and kind with others, demonstrating His great love. Ask God to cover the prayer requests of your seekers with His grace.

Care—Offer to help someone with a difficult or messy household task. Use the opportunity to help the person know you and God are there for him or her when he or she is not perfect.

Share—Share with your seekers times when you have disappointed God but realized He still loved you. Let them know when they make mistakes that God still loves them. He wants them to let Him show them how to live and love better.

Sail on Over to Day 6—Complete questions 7-9 of the review summary for day 6.

Charting My Course on Day 7—Based on today's reading, alter or add to your plan of action by charting your course on day 7.

Thought for the Day—We are called to be salt and light wherever we are.

DAY 4

Challenge Question—Do others ask you why you are so kind?
Review—Ps. 142:4

Jesus said, "Be holy, because I am holy" (1 Pet. 1:16). As Christians we are to be set apart from influences that separate us from the holy love of God. We are to be blameless in our lifestyle and holy in our conduct. As we walk closely with God, through the power of the Holy Spirit, we are able to shed the things that are not like Jesus. When we spend our time showing Him we love Him, He helps us do the things He desires and not do what displeases Him. Others will surely notice our transformed lives.

Since kindness is a rare trait these days, Christian kindness is a "showstopper." While traveling on an airplane my son Michael assisted an anxious elderly lady in telephoning her son to inform him of her delay. She asked Michael where he was headed. When he said to work at an evangelism festival, she said, "Oh, you're a Christian, so that is why you are so nice." People will know we are Christians by our love and kindness. It was true in the time of Jesus, it is true today, and it will be true tomorrow. You may never see the results of all your kind deeds, but God will. For this obedience He will pour out countless opportunities for others to see your witness of His love. If you are holy as God is holy, people will ask what makes you so kind. When they do this it is a wide-open door to share Christ!

Prayer—Ask God to make you holy as He is holy. Ask Him to show you any area of your life that you have not yet consecrated to Him. Pray that the Holy Spirit will continue guiding you to be His witness. Pray that the Spirit will prepare your seekers for your witnessing.

Care—Select an idea from your Care List that demonstrates God's love in action. What steps do you need to take to act on this?

Share—When others ask why you are so kind, be ready to tell them you are a follower of Jesus and it is He who has changed your actions and reactions.

Sail on Over to Day 6—Complete questions 10-12 of the review summary for day 6.

Charting My Course on Day 7—Based on today's reading, alter or add to your plan of action by charting your course on day 7.

Thought for the Day—People will know we are Christians by our love and kindness.

DAY 5

Challenge Question—Where are your seekers now?
Reread—Ps. 142:4

Your many acts of kindness are now making your seekers feel uncomfortable. Why? Because it is helping them grow closer to you and to God. As result they are beginning to feel vulnerable. They may also be experiencing the conviction of the Holy Spirit as they try to be like you in their own strength. As a result it is not uncommon for seekers to start making space, giving excuses, or using any kind of avoidance tactic to separate themselves from you. Remember, this is not a personal affront to you. A battle is raging within them between surrendering to God or continuing their present life. You are simply a messenger delivering plans to help God win the battle. Now more than ever, you must *not* quit witnessing.

Review Engel's Evangelistic Countdown for encouragement (Appendix H). Persevering in your witnessing at this point may make the difference between their surrendering to God or not. It is when we go the second, third, and fourth mile that seekers really see Jesus in us. Before they know He is real, they perceive Him as letting them down or being insufficient for their needs. Carefully explain that Jesus will never forsake them, even if you disappoint them somehow. This may cause them to persecute you, avoid you, or argue against you, but you must continue to bring them before the throne of God believing all things are possible. Remember the message of Luke 21:14-19: make up your mind beforehand to be willing to defend the truth, resist opponents, suffer isolation, endure hatred, because you will not perish. Scripture says our perseverance will gain lives. So press on for the higher calling of God in Christ Jesus. Blessings are around the corner. This perseverance is a test of your spiritual maturity and obedience.

Prayer—Ask God to bless those who persecute you and say false things about you. Ask Him to strengthen you for the battle. Continue to pray fervently for your seekers by name.

Care—Now more than ever, acts of care and kindness will testify to your seekers that God is living within you. Let Him show you what to do for others that will demonstrate that He will never leave them or forsake them. These acts of care will cost you something.

Share—Share with your seekers how God has caused you to go the extra mile where others fear to tread. Tell them being a good person is not enough to save us, but that we must be redeemed. Explain to them that God has provided the only way to heaven and an abundant, peaceful life.

Sail on Over to Day 6—Complete questions 13-15 of the review summary for day 6.

Charting My Course on Day 7—Based on today's reading, alter or add to your plan of action by charting your course on day 7.

Thought for the Day—Before the lost know Jesus is real, they perceive Him as letting them down or being insufficient for their needs.

DAY 6

Review Summary

Questions 1-15

1. Why is spiritual transformation the solution to impoverishment?

2. What social boundaries are you breaking in order to be a good, caring witness?

3. What ways can we foster security in our relationships?

4. How can you bring out the best in others?

5. To which of the following do your seekers respond best: kind words, acts of service, or quality time?

6. What are some good traits those you are praying for possess?

7. Why is remembering Rom. 3:23 important to our witness?

8. What ways have you demonstrated humble acts of kindness to your seekers?

9. Why is the encouragement of seekers so important when they make mistakes?

10. Why must Christians be holy people?

11. Why must seekers see our walk and hear our talk of Jesus?

12. Who has been impressed by your kindness this week?

13. Are your seekers starting to feel the conviction of God?

14. What will God help you do if you are persecuted?

15. What will God do if you are willing to suffer for His name's sake?

DAY 7

Charting My Course

Based on this week's readings, alter or add to your plan of action by charting your course.

	Name	Prayer Action	Care Action	Share Action	Prayer Answer
Day 1					
Day 2					
Day 3					
Day 4					
Day 5					
Day 6					
Day 7					

Week 7—A Guiding Lighthouse

DAY 1

Challenge Question—Who am I to guide others?

Read—Rom. 2:6-20

Action Item—Underline Rom. 2:19.

A good guidance counselor knows that offering choices of conduct and behavior, along with the consequences of each, will produce greater results than telling someone what they must do. As a guiding Lighthouse, you can use the same principle by showing the lost around you they have a choice: to continue to be lost, tossed to and fro, or to be found in the safe harbor. The choice is theirs. God desires so much for them to willingly choose Him, but He will not use force. He is glorified when we exercise the free will He gave us and follow Him. We can choose to go our own way, or we can choose to live life God's way.

Initially, everyone chooses his or her own way, which is rebellion against God. We "were like sheep going astray" (1 Pet. 2:25), but He provided the free gift of eternal life with Him. We must make the choice to receive this gift. Choosing God's way closes the separation between Him and us and results in obedience to Him and close fellowship with Him. His guidance for our lives is superior in all ways to our own, enabling us to enjoy abundant, joyful, and peaceful lives with Him. God promises "glory, honor and peace" to those who serve Him (Rom. 2:10).

As the Giver of every good and perfect gift, God has given us spiritual laws that enable us to follow Him. We must be doers of the laws of God, not just hearers only (James 1:22). We choose each day whether to defend and obey God's laws or deny them. Believers and nonbelievers alike will one day be judged according to their choices to obey or disobey God (Rom. 2:12-16). Believers, having chosen God's way, can be confident in being guides to the lost in the sea of life.

Prayer—Ask God to move in the hearts of those on your prayer list and cause them to desire to read His Word for specific guidance. Ask God to give you specific scriptures that you can direct your seekers to read.

Care—Maybe this would be a good time to give a Bible or evangelism resource that will help draw those on your prayer list to God. Many people do not have Bibles or biblical resources these days, and giving them something to care for their spiritual condition will be meaningful to them. (See Resources, Appendix J.)

Share—Ask those on your prayer list if they would be willing to read one or two scriptures along with you. Suggest key verses that relate to their needs, highlighting these verses for them in a Bible or other resource. Keep your discussions simple.

Sail on Over to Day 6—Complete questions 1-3 of the review summary for day 6.

Charting My Course on Day 7—Based on today's reading, alter or add to your plan of action by charting your course on day 7.

Thought for the Day—He is glorified when we follow Him by exercising the free will He gave us.

DAY 2

Challenge Question—If I have failures in my life, how can I guide others?

Read—Rom. 2:19

Action Item—Define the term *guide*.

Remember, we have all fallen short of God's glory (see Rom. 3:23). Having failed before or after our conversion experience does not determine whether we can guide well. This does not mean we have to backslide into sin after conversion. God is first interested in our redemption and then in our perfection. He is in the process of continually transforming every area of our lives to reflect Him. This is the sanctified life.

God through the Holy Spirit is able to perfect us every moment of every day if we will let Him. Being a good guidance counselor does not mean you have all the answers and have never made any mistakes yourself. In fact, some of the best counselors are those who have squarely acknowledged and confessed their own sins and shortcomings and have learned from them to help others. It is much easier to provide godly acceptance of others when we have acknowledged our own sinfulness.

God through His Son Jesus Christ is the Guide and Source of the light; we are the rays of light pointing to the Word, Spirit, and person of God as the *only* Guide to life.

Prayer—Ask God to use any of your failures as stepping-stones to share with unbelievers what He has done in your life. Confess any areas where you have been disobedient out of misplaced guilt or lack of confidence by neglecting to share the gospel. Bring your seekers' petitions to Him as well.

Care—Take the time to place the scriptures suggested for use when guiding seekers (Appendix D) in the back of your Bible for quick reference.

Share—Share willingly with your seekers any failures you may have had in your past and how God has redeemed your life.

Sail on Over to Day 6—Complete questions 4-6 of the review summary for day 6.

Charting My Course on Day 7—Based on today's reading, alter or add to your plan of action by charting your course on day 7.

Thought for the Day—God is first interested in our redemption and then in our perfection.

DAY 3

Challenge Question—What if I do not know how to guide?
Recite—Rom. 2:19
Action Item—Define the word *confident*.

Prov. 3:6 tells us that if we acknowledge Him in all our ways, He will make our paths straight. People have many different kinds of problems. The unbeliever has been walking apart from God's wisdom and has surely had many painful results. Although all problems have a spiritual dimension, not all problems are purely spiritual. Some people may have physical, mental, or emotional problems. Some may have financial, relational, or family issues. While salvation is our goal for them, there may be scriptural stepping-stone truths that uniquely apply to each of your seekers. These truths often speak to their hearts and sometimes will lead to actual conversion.

I strongly urge you to get a spiritual counseling resource book for your personal library (see Resources, Appendix J). A good resource will give a scriptural basis for most problems people encounter. Your pastor may have a good resource to help you, or you may contact me personally on the Internet at <www.outreachalert.org> with any questions you still have after covering this written material.

Two principles support confidence in sharing God's love: preparation and practice. As you are caring for those on your prayer list, you will encounter things that may be foreign to you. The most caring thing you can do for others is to prepare yourself with supportive resources in their areas of need. The next thing is to practice guiding seekers until it becomes easy. It was the same way when you first started to ride a bike. Remember how you had to prepare and practice? Your local Christian bookstore can lead you to resources that may fit a particular issue (i.e., blended families) that will help when you are witnessing. The Bible says, "If any of you lacks wisdom, he should ask God" (James 1:5).

Prayer—Pray the Lord will give you wisdom for your seekers. Praise Him for the answers to their prayer requests. Thank Him for how He has helped you in being a wise witness.

Care—Take photographs of your seekers' children on special events. Plan ahead to give them as gifts at just the right time.

Share—Share how important knowing God is when going through difficult times in our lives. Share how Jesus has made the way to salvation clear through His life on earth, and how we are to first repent and then respond to God in obedience. Share one area of your life before knowing Christ when you did not seek counsel from Him, and tell the outcome you suffered as a result.

Sail on Over to Day 6—Complete questions 7-9 of the review summary for day 6.

Charting My Course on Day 7—Based on today's reading, alter or add to your plan of action by charting your course on day 7.

Thought for the Day—"Trust in the LORD with all your heart and lean not on your own understanding; in all your ways acknowledge him, and he will make your paths straight" (Prov. 3:5-6).

DAY 4

Challenge Question—How should I be guiding a nonbeliever?
Read—Rom. 2:19

By now, your seekers know you are a Christian. They may know you go to church and read the Bible. But they may not have much knowledge of the fundamentals of the gospel that have changed your life. Now would be a good time to recheck Engel's Evangelistic Countdown and ask them where they are in their relationship with God. You might start a conversation with: "Tom, I have been sharing with you these past weeks about how God has taught me to love others, to be open about my faults, and to pray more effectively. I am wondering, what does God mean to you?"

When you do this, your seekers may or may not refer to Jesus in conjunction with God, depending on their spiritual background. If they refer to Jesus, then go on to ask them who He is to them. Listen carefully and intently without preaching. Thank them for sharing their views and casually mention that one day you would like to share who Jesus is to you. Unless the Spirit of God opens the door wider and moves them to ask you questions, leave it there. Let them think, reflect, and meditate on what they have said to you. Most people have never been asked these questions, so give them some time to answer. The Lord will stir in their hearts, and when they understand you care enough to want to know what they think, feel, and believe, you will have effectively started the guiding process. Remember, you are only accountable to lead them one step closer to knowing and following God—that is effective witnessing! Getting them to reflect is the first step.

Prayer—Ask God to show you clearly where your seekers are on their spiritual journey. Thank Him for the open doors to ask simple questions and learn more about them. Thank Him that He will work in their lives long after you have departed.

Care—Take great care in listening to where your seekers are spiritually. Let them express themselves even if days or weeks are needed.

Share—Confirm with your seekers that your acts of kindness, transparency, and prayer are a direct result of God teaching, moving, and guiding you. You are not seeking applause but are helping them understand the source of your strength and kindness.

Sail on Over to Day 6—Complete questions 10-12 of the review summary for day 6.

Charting My Course on Day 7—Based on today's reading, alter or add to your plan of action by charting your course on day 7.

Thought for the Day—"How, then, can they call on the one they have not believed in? And how can they believe in the one of whom they have not heard? And how can they hear without someone preaching to them?" (Rom. 10:14).

DAY 5

Challenge Question—Where are your seekers now?
Recite—Rom. 2:19

Taking the blinders of unbelief off unbelievers is a process. It may happen over time, or in minutes, depending upon their readiness. When you can effectively assess where your seekers are on their spiritual journey, you can know how and where to move them one step closer to a decision to follow Christ as Lord and Savior.

It has been said that witnessing is "One beggar telling another beggar where to find bread." You are responsible for the telling, not the response. Your seekers may be at the "rejection recycling point." They may believe there is a God, know what Christianity is, and have heard the word *gospel* but may have never understood the implications for their lives. If your seekers are still exhibiting positive attitudes toward you, they may be open to moving to the next step of admitting some of their problems, needs, or fears. Even if they are moving closer, every minute they wait, refuse, or disregard Jesus personally, they are still in a "rejection of the gospel" mode. They may even move back and forth for a time in this accepting/rejecting response. This is where your prayers must be sustained for them.

Often this is the point where many disciples give up on seekers. The reason? We all want to be liked and accepted. When we sense seekers are still rejecting God, we may take it personally. When we move away from seekers, nursing our own wounds and pride, we miss a vital point of potential instruction for which we have been praying and laboring. Do not take their rejection of God as a rejection of you.

Prayer—Ask the Lord to help you guide the seekers to the source of eternal life and leave the response between them and God. Ask Him to strengthen you to do your part, leaving His part to Him. Tell Him you would like to be reminded of the difference in order to stay focused.

Care—Continue to demonstrate special acts of kindness even when you feel rejected.

Share—Remind those on your prayer list that you will continue to be their friend even if they are "on the fence" in terms of a spiritual decision. Assure them of your love and ongoing acceptance. Your patience will speak volumes to them, letting them know that you really do know the truth.

Sail on Over to Day 6—Complete questions 13-15 of the review summary for day 6.

Charting My Course on Day 7—Based on today's reading, alter or add to your plan of action by charting your course on day 7.

Thought for the Day—Witnessing is "One beggar telling another beggar where to find bread."

DAY 6

Review Summary

Questions 1-15

1. Why does God give us a free will to decide whether or not to follow Him?

2. Why must we be doers of the laws of God, not just hearers?

3. Why are you a spiritual guide?

4. What is the sanctified life?

5. What will a wise guidance counselor do? What is his or her manual?

6. What do we have to do to have God make our paths straight?

7. What are the spiritual problems your seekers face?

8. Why is confidence important in witnessing for Christ?

9. Where can you find answers to some tough witnessing problems?

10. Why is awareness of a Supreme Being the first step in witnessing?

11. Can you name the other three steps between Supreme Being awareness and gospel fundamentals according to Engel's Evangelistic Countdown?

12. Why is it important to earn the right to explain who God is to you?

13. Review Engel's Evangelistic Countdown with each seeker in mind. What is the next step for each seeker?

14. When are we tempted to give up on seekers?

15. What issues are causing your seekers to stay "on the fence" in a salvation decision?

DAY 7

Charting My Course

Based on this week's readings, alter or add to your plan of action by charting your course.

	Name	Prayer Action	Care Action	Share Action	Prayer Answer
Day 1					
Day 2					
Day 3					
Day 4					
Day 5					
Day 6					
Day 7					

Week 8—A Strategizing Lighthouse

DAY 1

Challenge Question—How can I make the most of witnessing opportunities?

Read—Luke 12:35-42

Action Item—Define the word *readiness.*

We all have busy lives, but make the most of the opportunities God brings your way. Be open to others in their times of need and look for ways to extend a helping hand. Drop off an unexpected meal, or find ways to include unbelievers in your holiday gatherings. After sitting down to a meal and saying grace, take turns sharing what you are grateful for that God has supplied. This will demonstrate your faith in God and show others where your heart is.

Some believers invite college students from different countries to their homes during holiday weekends. Most foreign exchange students cannot afford to fly home for Christmas, so having a warm, welcoming home reflects to them the love and care of Jesus in a tangible way. Yes, it can be inconvenient for you as the host, but God will bless your stewardship and hospitality. Foreign students eventually go back to their countries having seen a real Christian up close and personal. What better way to be a missionary in your home?

Reaching out to seekers on their birthdays or on holidays will bring family traditions back to their minds. This gives them opportunities to share their traditions and family history with you, which will help you determine their spiritual needs. Listen very carefully to their backgrounds. Be ready to share your home and family times with the unsaved, sharing both bread and the Bread of Life. (See Lighthouse Christmas Party Packet in Appendix J, Resources.)

Prayer—Pray God will lead you to invite seekers into your home for specific events that will demonstrate the love and care of Christ. Thank Him for natural and comfortable opportunities to show your concern.

Care—Invite a seeker to your home for a holiday meal and take time to thank God for His goodness to you.

Share—Share with your seekers that they are welcome in your home and welcome to join your family. It will make them feel loved and wanted.

Sail on Over to Day 6—Complete questions 1-3 of the review summary for day 6.

Charting My Course on Day 7—Based on today's reading, alter or add to your plan of action by charting your course on day 7.

Thought for the Day—Be ready to share your home and family times with the unsaved, sharing both bread and the Bread of Life.

DAY 2

Challenge Question—How can I help when . . . ?
Read—Luke 12:37
Action Item—What does it mean to serve?

Everyone goes through painful life situations. Whether it is a family death, job loss, divorce, teen rebellion, or other causality, pain and hurt are conditions of life. How we move through those passages is an important part of our witness. We can become bitter, isolated, helpless, hopeless, anxious, and angry, or we can be forgiving, relational, proactive, hopeful, peaceful, and kind.

As we read His Word each day, God gives us instruction in the renewing of our minds. He helps us think good things if we allow Him. We can look at all things working for good, or we can look at the bleak side of things.

When we are hurting or struggling, we need to share how God is using these times for good and helping us overcome the pain. The painful times often tell just how close our friends really are to us. Struggles smoke out loyalty, trust, confidentiality, and truth. Some people avoid going to funeral homes because they do not know what to say to someone who is grieving. The mother of one of my seekers was dying and no one else would go with her to the hospital. Her friends were all afraid to deal with the reality of death. Friends who flee in times of need add to the pain of the hurting. We, too, will either be a part of the solution or a part of the problem for our seekers. Serving the needs of those who are in pain will afford many opportunities to share how God supplies our needs. Count the cost; it is worth every bit of your time, gifts, and energy.

Prayer—Thank God He has been with you through rough times in your life. Ask Him to help you be a caring servant to seekers who need a friend. Confess any attitudes you may have that are not pleasing to the Lord.

Care—Locate some special greeting cards in the bookstore with helpful scriptures on bereavement, illness, job loss, fear, weariness, or other types of needs; have these cards ready to send out immediately upon hearing of a seeker's need.

Share—Share with your friend some scripture verses that apply to his or her needs, such as Phil. 4:19. Make sure you explain what it means and where to locate it in the Bible.

Sail on Over to Day 6—Complete questions 4-6 of the review summary for day 6.

Charting My Course on Day 7—Based on today's reading, alter or add to your plan of action by charting your course on day 7.

Thought for the Day—Struggles smoke out loyalty, trust, confidentiality, and truth.

DAY 3

Challenge Question—What scripture do I give when . . . ?
Review—Luke 12:42

We should always be ready to give an answer for why the hope of Jesus is within us (1 Pet. 3:15). It is always wise to have scripture verses ready to guide seekers strategically to the Bible to meet their needs. They may not have the habit of doing so. If we never open God's Word, to show seekers it is our source of strength, they will never open it either. While we cannot always have the scripture in our memory bank that fits the specific need, we can place in the back of our Bibles a reference list of key scriptures commonly used when guiding seekers. Here are some common scriptures I have used:

I am too bad for God (Luke 18:9-14).
I cannot live the Christian life (Isa. 41:10).
I fear ridicule (Luke 12:4-5).
I may lose my job (Mark 8:36).
I cannot give up ____ in my life (Gal. 5:19-21).
I only see hypocrites (Rom. 14:13).
I cannot forgive (Matt. 6:15; Phil. 4:13).
I am in grief (Matt. 5:4).
I need guidance (Prov. 3:5-6).
I need peace (John 14:27).
I am tempted (1 Cor. 10:13).
I am weary (1 Pet. 5:6-7).

Do not bombard seekers with too many scripture verses at once. Keep your references simple and strategic. You might look up each one of these passages in your Bible and tab or highlight each for quick reference. You will be glad you can give "meat" when others only give "scraps." Give them these rations at the right time.

Prayer—Thank God for His Word that never returns void. Thank Him that Scripture cuts to our hearts and souls like double-edged sword. Ask Him to bring verses to mind that will be timely food for thought for your seekers.

Care—Take the time to highlight scriptures that can be understood and located easily in times of need.

Share—Call or send a note this week to one of your seekers, sharing a scripture that fits his or her need.

Sail on Over to Day 6—Complete questions 7-9 of the review summary for day 6.

Charting My Course on Day 7—Based on today's reading, alter or add to your plan of action by charting your course on day 7.

Thought for the Day—We should always be ready to give an answer for why the hope of Jesus is within us (1 Pet. 3:15).

DAY 4

Challenge Question—How can I know my caring is working?

Recite—Luke 12:42

Action Item—Define the term *stewardship*.

Seizing the opportunities God gives us to witness is sensible, worth modeling, and blessed according to Luke 12:42. We can squander God's gift of time or use it wisely.

Being a good steward means that we must determine what to give, when to give, how much to give, and to whom we give. Scripture reminds us to "not become weary in doing good, for at the proper time we will reap" (Gal. 6:9). We may never see the reward of our faithful stewardship until we get to heaven. Giving may cause us to suffer persecution, financial loss, the judgment of others, ingratitude, or even to lose our lives, as Jesus did. We may never know if our acts of kindness have any meaning for others. Think of how many people never returned to thank Jesus for His healing, but we can know that if we give to others out of a heart of love for God, He will bless our giving and will not forget.

Our motivation to give and to be a good steward of what God has given us must be out of complete obedience to Him. God still blesses the obedient and punishes the disobedient. You will one day give an account for the gifts He has given you and how wisely you used them for Kingdom expansion. By seeing consistent acts of thoughtful kindness, seekers may begin to emulate your kind behavior. When those you have prayed for start giving back to you, you will know your care is working. Be sure to allow your seekers the opportunity to give and show special kindness to you. If you do not, you will deny them blessings. The greatest compliment your friends can give you is to pass along to others in need the generosity you have shown them.

"Every good and perfect gift" comes from our Father (James 1:17). He does not give gifts for us to hoard selfishly. He has given them in full measure to be faithfully used for His purposes. If you have not yet discovered the ways God has uniquely gifted you, take time to learn and put these gifts to Kingdom use.

Prayer—Thank God for the many gifts He has given you. Ask Him to show you how to be a good steward of the gifts He has given you for His glory. If you are uncertain what gifts He has given you, ask Him to reveal them to you.

Care—Use one of your spiritual gifts this week to encourage a seeker.

Share—Look for areas where God has gifted your seekers. By your example, challenge them to turn those gifts over to Him. Look for ways to let your seekers know that your giftedness comes from God and not from yourself.

Sail on Over to Day 6—Complete questions 10-12 of the review summary for day 6.

Charting My Course on Day 7—Based on today's reading, alter or add to your plan of action by charting your course on day 7.

Thought for the Day—Being a good steward means that we must determine what to give, when to give, how much to give, and to whom we give.

DAY 5

Challenge Question—Where are your seekers now?
Read—Luke 12:42
Action Item—Define *faithfulness*.

This week you have been examining ways to use the gifts God has given you to further the goals of the Great Commission (Matt. 28:19-20). You may have discovered your home can be used in outreach, how to take spiritual advantage of distressing life events, scriptures to use when guiding a seeker, or how to be a good steward of your gifts in obedience to God. All of these lessons require faithfulness on your part to cultivate over a lifetime.

Caring gets the attention of the seeker. By now you have gotten your seekers' attention with acts of kindness, and they know the care comes from the Lord. They should feel very special to have received His favor through you. They should respond positively toward you and be taking steps of vulnerable confession. They should be primed for the big "D"—Decision. Witnessing your Christian life should convict them that they need Jesus too. They will understand faith as you are faithful to them. They will understand repentance when you openly share how you rebelled against God before you came to know and follow Him personally. Your demeanor of sorrow over your past life before Christ should model the sorrow they should feel over being separated from Him as well. At this point seekers are starting to realize they are in a battle between God's will for their lives and their own will. Find ways to gently point out those areas of God's plan for their lives that differ from theirs. When they suffer the consequences of poor choices, faithfully point out how God has provided a way out of their mess. Be faithful in the little points of instructing and in due time you will reap a harvest.

Prayer—Thank God for the many ways He has given you to show His care to others. Ask Him to keep you faithful in reaching out to others with acts of kindness. Pray that He would so move in the hearts of your seekers that they would see your good works and glorify your Father in heaven.

Care—Take great care to foster even small admissions of shortcomings to allow seekers to see that when they do fall you still accept and love them as Jesus would.

Share—Remind your seekers that all have sinned and need God's grace. Humble yourself with public confessions so that seekers can know Jesus desires every area of our lives to be under His blood of redemption. Share that God is not finished helping you mature spiritually either.

Sail on Over to Day 6—Complete questions 13-15 of the review summary for day 6.

Charting My Course on Day 7—Based on today's reading, alter or add to your plan of action by charting your course on day 7.

Thought for the Day—Caring gets the attention of the seeker.

DAY 6

Review Summary

Questions 1-15

1. How can you open your home for witnessing opportunities?

2. What does it mean to be a good steward of your time?

3. To what specific events at church or elsewhere can you take seekers where the gospel is clearly presented?

4. What does it mean in Luke 12:37 (NASB) to be "on the alert"?

5. Who are we to serve?

6. How can pain be an open door to witnessing?

7. Why is scripture important to effective witnessing?

8. Why is it important to model the use of scriptures?

9. What scriptures have you used for meeting needs?

10. What does being a good steward mean?

11. Why is it important to receive as well as give?

12. What are three gifts God has given you for His glory?

13. What are the five action words in Matt. 28:19-20?

14. Why is faithfulness important in witnessing?

15. Where are your seekers now on Engel's Evangelistic Countdown? If they are not starting to be at the confessing stage, what should you do?

DAY 7

Charting My Course

Based on this week's readings, alter or add to your plan of action by charting your course.

	Name	Prayer Action	Care Action	Share Action	Prayer Answer
Day 1					
Day 2					
Day 3					
Day 4					
Day 5					
Day 6					
Day 7					

Week 9—A Preparing Lighthouse

DAY 1

Challenge Question—What do I need to learn?

Read—1 Pet. 3:15

Action Item—Identify the main verbs in the text for today.

Effective witnessing requires sharing a holy heart of love with those without Christ (Acts 1:8, 31). Effective witnessing requires that we are ready to tell about the hope, peace, and joy we enjoy as believers. Effective witnessing gives detailed steps to a seeker on how to receive Christ personally and totally. Our attitude and motivation must be grounded in love and concern for the seeker.

If we feel a seeker isn't making a decision for Christ soon enough and we become pushy, harsh, wordy, or anxious about the decision, he or she will feel pressured and may reject Him as a result. It may take him or her months or even years to choose Christ. There is nothing we can do to speed up the process.

We can, however, be ready to give a complete, effective, and comprehensive gospel presentation. Just as common steps to going on a trip include washing clothes, purchasing needed items, and packing, in witnessing our hearts must be clean, our Bible verses or resources must be acquired, and we must have "witnessing tools" available. It has been said if we fail to plan, we plan to fail. This week will focus on the preparation for a successful excursion in witnessing. Let's prepare to power up our Lighthouses!

Prayer—Ask God to help as you prepare to share the gospel effectively. Ask Him to give you wisdom in what skills you may need to learn or refresh. Pray for your seekers by name.

Care—Purchase greeting cards that present the gospel, and have them ready as needed.

Share—Share with your accountability partner your need of prayer for diligence in preparation to effectively witness.

Sail on Over to Day 6—Complete questions 1-3 of the review summary for day 6.

Charting My Course on Day 7—Based on today's reading, alter or add to your plan of action by charting your course on day 7.

Thought for the Day—If we fail to plan, we plan to fail.

DAY 2

Challenge Question—How can I know someone is ready to receive Christ?

Read—1 Pet. 3:15

When you maintain a good relationship with those on your Lighthouse prayer list, they will be open to your sharing Christ on some level. Some may even feel they are humoring you by listening to your witness. Seekers will often send out signals confirming that they are ready to make a decision. They might respond well to you by beginning to use religious references in their conversations. References to God, Jesus, church, or prayer are examples that demonstrate their closeness to conversion. They may leave their Bible out for you to notice or may start attending church. Some will want to discuss their religious background with you to let you know that they are searching. Others will be very candid and tell you they are needing answers to spiritual questions. A readiness signal prior to conversion is that seekers move closer to other Christians.

Another sign that your seekers may be encountering God is that they may feel uncomfortable around you as the Holy Spirit is drawing them closer to God. This often means they are under His convicting and convincing power. Remember, all of us know where we are on our spiritual journeys. We just need to acknowledge it to God and allow Him to bring us closer to himself. It is your gentle accepting spirit at this point that will allow seekers to be totally honest with you and God. If you ask Him, the Holy Spirit will go before you as you relate to seekers.

Prayer—Thank God for allowing you to maintain a loving relationship with your seekers. Ask God to show you ways your seekers are moving closer to Him, and pray for the Holy Spirit to go before you as you encourage your seekers to take the next step.

Care—Review Engel's Evangelistic Countdown and pinpoint where you think each of your seekers is on the scale.

Share—Share with your seekers your joy over the steps they are taking and that they are talking about the things of God. Encourage, encourage, encourage!

Sail on Over to Day 6—Complete questions 4-6 of the review summary for day 6.

Charting My Course on Day 7—Based on today's reading, alter or add to your plan of action by charting your course on day 7.

Thought for the Day—"But you will receive power when the Holy Spirit comes on you; and you will be my witnesses in Jerusalem, and in all Judea and Samaria, and to the ends of the earth" (Acts 1:8).

DAY 3

Challenge Question—What tools can help me share?
Read—1 Pet. 3:15
Action Item—Define the term *spiritual preparedness.*

If you were to make a list of all the objects in your home, it might take you months. Have you ever considered how many of those objects are useful to God's purposes? Just look around you for a moment. We have a tendency to accumulate material objects. Think about what things in your home could help you share your faith—family photos, Bible, devotionals, pictures with scripture. All these things say God is important in your life.

To be well prepared for the good work of the Great Commission there are also some essential objects to have close at hand. Review this list and make sure you are prepared to use these things:

- Bible—in a translation easy for nonbelievers to understand, with salvation passages highlighted.
- Gospel outline—have an outline of scripture verses presented in a simple clear manner (see Appendix F).
- Tracts—acquire these visual tools for easy, simple gospel presentations in any setting.
- Basic Bible Studies—essential follow-up for new believers in their first days of conversion (Appendix G).
- Your personal testimony—first have this written out, then memorized and practiced for presentation at any time (Appendix E).
- Personal business cards or 3" x 5" cards to give seekers your contact information.
- Gospel greeting cards—available for any seeker's need.
- Christian books—on topics of interest to nonbelievers (i.e., blended families).
- Kleenex—handy for tears of repentance.
- Pen—be ready to write down information such as telephone numbers and the date of a first Bible study meeting.

Prayer—Pray for God to prompt you to become prepared to witness in any circumstance.

Care—Take time to purchase and assemble the suggested items to have on hand. Make sure you carry your favorite tracts with you in your purse or wallet. Be prepared for the open doors God gives you for sharing.

Share—Share with your accountability partner ways you have prepared better for witnessing since you began *Lighting the Way.* Have him or her share some witnessing tips that may be useful yet different from yours.

Sail on Over to Day 6—Complete questions 7-9 of the review summary for day 6.

Charting My Course on Day 7—Based on today's reading, alter or add to your plan of action by charting your course on day 7.

Thought for the Day—"These commandments that I give you today are to be upon your hearts. . . . Write them on the doorframes of your houses and on your gates" (Deut. 6:6, 9).

DAY 4

Challenge Question—Where can I go for help with tough witnessing questions?
Read—1 Pet. 3:15

Sometimes the difference between a person who commits suicide and a person who works through devastating circumstances is the presence of hope. Hope gives people a reason to try again, to try differently. Hope helps people believe in the possibility that tomorrow can be different. People who do not find their hope in Christ look to less fulfilling places to find it. They may place their hope in financial security, in family, or in their own abilities. When people hope in something that is unstable or changeable, they live in hopelessness without even knowing it. The hope we find in Jesus transcends all other sources of hope. It is more than wishful thinking. Faith in salvation through Christ creates hope for any situation.

While sharing hope is a privilege, there may be many life circumstances nonbelievers face for which we have no point of reference. For example, we may never have faced a significant job loss, divorce, or a family member who converts to a cult. What can we do in these tough witnessing situations to offer hope? Who can help? Unique situations often require unique preparation. Your church pastoral staff, Christian bookstore, local Christian radio station, Christian counseling centers, evangelistic proclamation ministry personnel, and large parachurch ministries like Focus on the Family all have support resources and staff to help you when your seekers experience unique problems. I, too, am available at <www.outreachalert.org> to answer any questions that arise. Specific resources outlined in Appendix J will also assist you. When you encounter such difficult situations in witnessing, seek counsel from trusted leaders who will steer you in the right direction and be prepared to share the Source of your hope!

Prayer—Ask God to reveal any special circumstances in the lives of your seekers for which you need to be prepared to offer hope.
Care—Take time to acquire resources on topics your seekers may be struggling with, and send them hopeful materials to help.
Share—Be sure to offer your seekers resources that present a clear gospel message and guidance for special circumstances. When you hear the word *hope* in casual conversations, use it to transition to a discussion of why *true hope* is more than wishful thinking.

Sail on Over to Day 6—Complete questions 10-12 of the review summary for Day 6.

Charting My Course on Day 7—Based on today's reading, alter or add to your plan of action by charting your course on day 7.

Thought for the Day—Hope gives people a reason to try again, to try differently.

DAY 5

Challenge Question—Am I prepared?
Read—1 Pet. 3:15

Many Christians want to believe that people will identify them as Christians just by the life they lead. While you have been exercising many caring gestures toward those on your prayer list, ask yourself if it is enough for your seekers to just see your walk and not hear you talk about your experience with Christ. Loving acts evaporate when there are no words to confirm them. The Bible says we must give an answer for our hope. That means we must walk and talk about our joy in Christ so others will know our peace comes from Him and not from ourselves. Put aside your fear of failure, rejection, or inconvenience to share the words about your life in Christ. Being a well-maintained Lighthouse means being well prepared to give verbal answers.

Having the tools ready to help you talk about your faith is essential. A small visual tool like a picture or tract will help you walk through the steps to finding peace with God. A visual tool is good for both your seekers' memory and yours. People will remember a picture and forget a thousand words. In addition to preparing for preconversions we must prepare for postconversions.

Approximately 50 percent of newborn Christians fall away from God because no one disciples them (*Conserve the Converts,* 14). A new Christian needs the assistance of a mature believer within the first 24 hours of conversion—the same way a newborn needs a parent. Having a tool ready in the basics of the walk of faith is vital. A simple eight-week Bible study for 30 to 60 minutes once a week covering prayer, Bible study, church attendance, fellowship, giving, and witnessing will build lasting disciples (see Appendix G). This is a good time to assess your readiness to share the words of the gospel with a nonbeliever. You don't have to have all the verses memorized; just have a tract to get started. It is no more sacred to share the gospel without the help of tools than with them.

Prayer—Ask God to open doors for you to begin sharing your faith in Christ, using your witnessing tools.

Care—Remember to have your witnessing tools handy to give away.

Share—Look for ways to talk about your "great Christ" rather than your "good day."

Sail on Over to Day 6—Complete questions 13-15 of the review summary for day 6.

Charting My Course on Day 7—Based on today's reading, alter or add to your plan of action by charting your course on day 7.

Thought for the Day—Being a well-maintained Lighthouse means being well prepared to give verbal answers.

DAY 6

Review Summary

Questions 1-15

1. What three components are important for effective witnessing?

2. What may happen if your attitude and conduct are not godly?

3. Why must a gospel presentation be clear, complete, and concise?

4. What signals, if any, are your seekers sending that they may be close to making a decision for Christ?

5. Where are your seekers on their spiritual journey?

6. Why is Acts 1:8 essential to this stage of witnessing?

7. What are spiritual tools?

8. Do you have any items you need to remove from your home to make it a better witness?

9. What tools do you need to acquire to be ready to share your faith with ease?

10. Who on your prayer list needs hope?

11. What resources can you share that will show your seekers how hope in Jesus can change their world forever?

12. In what ways can you convey that hope in Jesus protects you from unnecessary fear and dread?

13. Why must we walk and talk our faith in Christ?

14. What is meant by a "well-prepared Lighthouse"?

15. What will happen if new converts do not receive follow-up with Bible studies?

DAY 7

Charting My Course

Based on this week's readings, alter or add to your plan of action by charting your course.

	Name	Prayer Action	Care Action	Share Action	Prayer Answer
Day 1					
Day 2					
Day 3					
Day 4					
Day 5					
Day 6					
Day 7					

Week 10—A Customizing Lighthouse

DAY 1

Challenge Question—Why is sharing necessary?

Read—John 12:35-36

Action Item—Consciously start putting trust in the Light.

Sharing the love, forgiveness, redemption, and gift of eternal life known only in a personal relationship with Jesus Christ has happened consistently since Pentecost. Yet, today a healthy fear of the Lord has generally been replaced by a religion of self-worship. Since "self" makes all the choices and judgments in so many people's lives, who is there to fear? As Christians our lives must be heralding others to restore their relationship with and awe of the holy God. We must underscore in our own lives a holy desire to know God so that others will strive to know Him. We must show *and* tell.

Jesus warns us that we will not have His light unless we walk in the Light. He has given us His light to see the path of loving Him and others completely. We can never become the sons and daughters of light unless we obey the teachings of God each day. He taught us to pass on to others the light that only He can give. When I came to trust Christ as Lord and Savior, it was as if He turned on a light in the midst of a very dark room. I could see Him as never before. The light of Jesus brought the dawn of a new day for me. The ability to give seekers a sense of God's presence is only bestowed upon the children of light.

Prayer—Ask God to help you be a strong link in the chain of sharing the gospel as it has been since Pentecost. Ask Him to help you identify anything in your life that you have not given totally to Him.

Care—Exercise one care item for each seeker from your Care List this week.

Share—Find a way to share with one of your seekers what it means to have a healthy fear of God in your own life. Use a picture of a lighthouse to describe how God gives us light for our lives.

Sail on Over to Day 6—Complete questions 1-3 of the review summary for day 6.

Charting My Course on Day 7—Based on today's reading, alter or add to your plan of action by charting your course on day 7.

Thought for the Day—We must show and tell others about the grace of God.

DAY 2

Challenge Question—What are ways I can share my faith effectively?

Read—John 12:35-36

Action Item—Complete the Personal Testimony Work Sheet (Appendix E).

We are living in a culture that is increasingly hostile. In this environment a kind word and deed can demonstrate God's love in action and defuse hostility. Sometimes we may think we have to be civil engineers in order to build bridges of love to nonbelievers. Yet, love is our strongest "defense" and our best "offense" to people in an unbelieving world. The love of God never fails; it is the light for today's cynical world. As His disciples we will be increasingly tested to share His love. If we do not obey the command of Jesus in preaching and teaching others to obey Him, we, too, will have something to fear. When we have built bridges into the lives of others by praying and caring for their needs, we must be ready to clearly share how we can remain hopeful, loving, kind, and forgiving in a rebellious world.

Use the work sheet for your personal testimony (Appendix E) and write out a three-minute version. Tell of your life before Christ. Use a key scripture as your theme. Explain what happened when you came to trust Christ. And then joyfully give some detail about how your life has been different since that time. Keep your testimony short. This should not be your life story. Make your seekers want to hear more. Use a life theme, such as your lack of peace before Christ, and give your favorite scripture on the peace of God that caused you to turn from sin, and finally, discuss the peace you have with God today. Be specific. Avoid confusing words and religious language like *denominations, salvation,* or *regeneration.* Practice giving your personal testimony with your accountability partner. Take plenty of time to develop your personal testimony. You may be called upon for a shorter or longer version. Be prepared.

Prayer—Ask God to help you form a clear personal testimony so that others may know and follow Jesus Christ.

Care—Take great care and time to formulate your personal testimony.

Share—Share your personal testimony with your accountability partner and your family. Let them help you refine it to be clear and concise. Share it with another Christian for practice and assurance of clarity.

Sail on Over to Day 6—Complete questions 4-6 of the review summary for day 6.

Charting My Course on Day 7—Based on today's reading, alter or add to your plan of action by charting your course on day 7.

Thought for the Day—Love is our strongest "defense" and our best "offense" for people in an unbelieving world.

DAY 3

Challenge Question—What are nonthreatening ways to share the gospel?

Read—John 12:35-36

Action Item—Identify the action words in the text for today.

We may not all give our witness of the love of God the same way. We are all uniquely gifted by God for the purpose of Kingdom growth. If we claim we do not have the gift to witness, we are denying the gospel that lives within us.

As noted on Engel's Evangelistic Countdown, there are many steps people may take before fully trusting the Lord Jesus. It may take years for some to be ready to make a decision for Christ. Many people may play a part in the process. Other seekers may be ready to accept Christ immediately. We must keep our eyes off the outcome of salvation and focus on the process. In addition to prayer, care, and sharing our personal testimony, it is beneficial to take seekers to church or Christian events where the gospel is clearly presented. Or your family may drop off a *JESUS* video or some other clear gospel message and then discuss it later with seekers. The NeedHim short radio features heard nationally are also good ways to communicate the gospel to your seekers in nonthreatening ways. Just ask them to tune in at a given time and let you know what they think. Several proclamation ministries like the Billy Graham Evangelistic Association or Luis Palau Evangelistic Association have web sites that are good vehicles for seekers who are Internet users. Many ministry and book resources are available that appeal to many needs and walk through the steps of salvation. (See Resources, Appendix J.) Use your favorite gospel tract and guide seekers through each step yourself. (See Tips on Using a Gospel Tract, Appendix I.) Tracts are:

- easy to follow
- good to refer to later at a less emotional time
- flexible to return to earlier steps when someone gets stalled
- foster questions
- make "step" transitions smoother
- help seekers know others have had the same spiritual journey, and
- assure them you will come to an end in your presentation

Prayer—Ask God to help you be patient with all of the steps it may take for your seekers to come to trust Him. Ask for insight in how to continue to encourage your seekers.

Care—Choose a care item from your Care List and implement it this week.

Share—Use with your seekers one of the ways to share the gospel that were discussed in your study today, or use another idea you may have. Ask them for a response.

Sail on Over to Day 6—Complete questions 7-9 of the review summary for day 6.

Charting My Course on Day 7—Based on today's reading, alter or add to your plan of action by charting your course on day 7.

Thought for the Day—We are all uniquely gifted by God for the purpose of Kingdom growth.

DAY 4

Challenge Question—How do I share my faith with those different from me?

Action Item—Recite John 12:35-36.

Did you know that thousands of people permanently leave our churches each week? It is very obvious that the world is groping for answers to their hopelessness, yet many feel they are not good enough to attend church or that only hypocrites go there. When we receive Jesus as our Lord and Savior we receive His love for all kinds of people, some very different from ourselves. If we do not have passion for Christ and others, we will not have the power of God, for it is the Holy Spirit's power that seeks and saves the lost (Acts 1:8).

When we drink deeply of the life of Jesus, we will give out deeply, especially to those who are different. For example, people drawn to cults may be offensive to us, but we must methodically continue to expose them to scriptural truth. They may test our Christian conduct—to be sure we really do have an edge on truth and light—and must be taught intensely over long periods of time. We may experience other differences that challenge us to find common ground with seekers, such as religious backgrounds, ethnic diversity, social and cultural diversity, as well as age differences. Our personal testimony can be modified to bridge the similarities we have with others and minimalize the differences.

In the area of rebellion against God there are no differences among people. Isa. 53:6 reminds us that in the matter of sin, "All of us like sheep have gone astray" (NASB). Being partners with God in the conversion birth process may be long and exhausting, but it is well worth the effort and sacrifice of our time and energy.

Prayer—Ask God for an open door to find common ground with someone very different from you. Ask Him to mold you to respond to differences as He would. Confess any prejudice you may have.

Care—Look for a special way to celebrate the diversity of your seekers, such as enjoying an ethnic meal together.

Share—If seekers speak a second language, learn some loving, affirming expressions in their language to let them know you care about them. Tell them about your family traditions and build a bridge into their lives. Share that Jesus is known among all people and that He cares for every one of us. (See Resources, Appendix J.)

Sail on Over to Day 6—Complete questions 10-12 of the review summary for day 6.

Charting My Course on Day 7—Based on today's reading, alter or add to your plan of action by charting your course on day 7.

Thought for the Day—When we receive Jesus as our Lord and Savior we receive His love for all kinds of people, some very different from ourselves.

DAY 5

Challenge Question—Where are your seekers now?
Read—John 12:35-36
Action Item—Why must the Son of Man be lifted up?

Holy Spirit heat is being turned up on your seekers now. At first they were amazed by your godly love, then they realized why you are so loving, and then they realized the consequences of this love for their own lives. Tough seeker questions may now be coming with vigor (Appendix D). Signs of discontent, agitation, and guilt may be surfacing in your seekers. Do you remember how masked these signs were when you first started praying for them? Like a rose, the petals are folding back to reveal their vulnerable souls to you. Be careful and gentle, yet firm on where you stand. They may or may not realize their hearts are bending in God's direction. The Light is drawing them. Treat them as if they were already saved and living for God. This regard will subtly increase their confidence to make the leap from faith in themselves to the faith in the God they have been avoiding. By your actions, let them know there is safety on the other side of the leap. Continue to practice using the tools suggested to prepare for the open door God brings for you to share the words of the Giver of light. Congratulations! You've obediently prepared your Lighthouse for *Lighting the Way.*

Prayer—Ask God to help you stand firm as you lovingly help each of your seekers feel emotionally safe with you and open to the next spiritual step.

Care—Be especially sensitive to your seekers' emotional needs.

Share—Share with your seekers a few of the nonthreatening ways suggested to let them hear the words and implications of the gospel for the first time. Remember, anything worth saying once is worth saying 16 times in different ways in order to help your seekers understand. Use all means available, and do not be afraid to repeat yourself.

Sail on Over to Day 6—Complete questions 13-15 of the review summary for day 6.

Charting My Course on Day 7—Based on today's reading, alter or add to your plan of action by charting your course on day 7.

Thought for the Day—"Put your trust in the light while you have it, so that you may become sons of light" (John 12:36).

DAY 6

Review Summary

Questions 1-15

1. Why is a healthy fear of God important to a healthy spiritual walk?

2. How do we demonstrate that we are sons and daughters of light to a dark world?

3. What must we do to become sons and daughters of light?

4. What will happen to us if we do not obey Christ's command to share our faith?

5. What are the three components of a short personal testimony? (See Appendix E.)

6. Why should we avoid religious words or unfamiliar terms with nonbelievers?

7. Where are your seekers on Engel's Evangelistic Countdown?

8. What are some nonthreatening ways the gospel can be communicated in addition to your personal testimony?

9. Why are tracts nonthreatening, useful tools?

10. Where do we get the power to be effective witnesses?

11. Why do people involved in cults need lots of scriptural exposure?

12. In what ways are all people alike?

13. Why is discontentment, agitation, or guilt starting to surface in the lives of your seekers?

14. Why is sensitivity toward emotional needs important?

15. Are there any witnessing areas in which you are not prepared? If so, shore them up by praying, studying, and practicing your witnessing.

DAY 7

Charting My Course

Based on this week's readings, alter or add to your plan of action by charting your course.

	Name	Prayer Action	Care Action	Share Action	Prayer Answer
Day 1					
Day 2					
Day 3					
Day 4					
Day 5					
Day 6					
Day 7					

Week 11—A Resisting Lighthouse

DAY 1

Challenge Question—Who shared with me and how did it work?

Read—Isa. 52:7

Action Item—Identify five blessings we are to share with others.

Take a walk down memory lane. Do you remember the name of the person who first shared the gospel with you? What was that person like? How did he or she reach you in ways that spoke to your heart? What words did that person use to make the gospel clear in your mind? Whatever God used, through the Holy Spirit, to personalize himself and make you turn from rebelling against Him, the fact is that someone shared His love with you and helped you clearly see your need.

Just as wise parents recall their growing-up struggles in order to better understand how they can be better parents, you are wise to remember your own spiritual journey while spiritually parenting the unconverted or recently converted. Remember how stubborn you were before believing in God's love? Were you challenging, resistant, rebellious, slow, or even derogatory to the things of God? Recalling your own journey helps you be steadfast in sharing God's love. You can be appropriately compassionate yet decisively urgent in your witness to the lost. Just as teenagers give their parents a hard time, your seekers will give you a hard time. Expect it and you'll be prepared. Remember your past, and it will keep you humble in sharing the gospel.

Prayer—Ask God to remind you of your own life without Him to be more sensitive to know how and when to share the words of the gospel with your seekers.

Care—From your Care List, select one idea for this week to use for your seekers.

Share—Share with your accountability partner your own spiritual journey to remind you both of the salvation process. Share with your partner how you need prayer to be "on time" for God's appointment in the lives of your seekers.

Sail on Over to Day 6—Complete questions 1-3 of the review summary for day 6.

Charting My Course on Day 7—Based on today's reading, alter or add to your plan of action by charting your course on day 7.

Thought for the Day—Recalling your own journey helps you be steadfast in sharing God's love. You can be appropriately compassionate yet decisively urgent in your witness to the lost.

DAY 2

Challenge Question—Why am I distracted when presenting the gospel?

Read—Isa. 52:7

Action Item—Underline the first 14 words of the text for today.

We have often heard the biblical phrase "how beautiful are the feet of those who bring the good news" (Rom. 10:15), but what does it mean? It is a reference to messengers who ran from the scene of battle to bring news of the outcome to a waiting king and people. In this passage, "news" refers to the Israelites' return from exile and deliverance found in God. The reason we are often distracted from sharing the gospel after much preparation is that we are in a spiritual battle. The devil is prowling around, upset because you are victoriously sharing the Good News that will set another soul free from his control. This is a front-line attack.

I recall once while witnessing to someone on a patio that I was swarmed by bees. Not long after that the children started acting up, the TV was blaring, and the phone started ringing. I wondered when I would get to the point of sharing the steps of salvation and obedience to God. The best response to attacks when sharing the Good News is to pray away the evil one, keep your focus, and defeat the enemy by continuing to boldly share. If you are prepared for this to be a point of contention, you will also be prepared to tough it out through any distraction or obstacle. This battle is a sign you are right on track in presenting the words to set your seekers free. *Do not give up!* Keep presenting the gospel. Even if circumstances seem to delay you, return to the point of presentation. (See Gospel Outline, Appendix F.) Do not move off course, even if it means having to share again days later. Be a strong and courageous Lighthouse. Send out clear, radiant beams of light in the midst of darkness. Beacon your seekers to safe harbor (Appendix F) if they are ready to make a decision.

Prayer—Pray God will protect you from giving in to the forces coming against your witness, against your clear presentation of the gospel, and against the receptive hearts of your seekers.

Care—Regardless of your seekers' response to your witness, keep on demonstrating care and love.

Share—Using the tracts, your written gospel presentation, or another tool, find a quiet, private location with one of your seekers and begin sharing the steps to finding peace, joy, love, and the forgiveness of God. (See Gospel Outline, Appendix F.)

Sail on Over to Day 6—Complete questions 4-6 of the review summary for day 6.

Charting My Course on Day 7—Based on today's reading, alter or add to your plan of action by charting your course on day 7.

Thought for the Day—"Put on the full armor of God so that you can take your stand against the devil's schemes" (Eph. 6:11).

DAY 3

Challenge Question—What makes sharing the gospel take hold?

Read—Isa. 52:7 (concluding phrase)

Action Item—Say aloud, "My God reigns!"

The Father, Son, and Holy Spirit cause the Good News to take deep root in the lives of persons genuinely searching for God. Anyone who calls on God's name will find Him, yet good teaching, obedience modeling, review, encouragement, and continual godly love from you will help ensure your seekers' long-term spiritual victory. You may have to repeat biblical truths over and over, or you may have to revisit *the steps* to finding God's peace. If the gospel-sharing process stalls, you may have to reignite the fire. But when all is said and done, the battle is ultimately fought between God and the forces of evil. It is His battle, and the best news is He wins! Even if it does not seem so now, your seekers one day will bow in reverence to your holy God. It may be now or sadly later, but it will occur.

As other believers lift those on your prayer list in prayer, reinforcing the love of God and His attributes, your seekers' obedience to Him will come more quickly. You want your seekers to know the joy of serving your Lord and Master while they are alive (immediately and fully). A good time to start praying for the results of their conversion is before they make the decision to follow Christ. Prayer and initial follow-up after conversion are also part of the witnessing process. Although you may share the words of the gospel, your seekers may pray the prayer of salvation and then the next day be unsure of their commitment. Basic assurance Bible studies (see Appendix G) are part of the responsible witnessing process. Only when seekers are fully grounded and obedient to God should you let up in teaching the discipline of sharing what God has done and is doing in their lives.

Prayer—Ask God to keep you faithful in doing your part for the witnessing process, and thank Him for doing His part as He has promised.

Care—Lovingly set up times when you and a seeker can go through Bible studies for new or growing believers. (See Appendixes F and G, Basic Bible Studies and Gospel Outline.)

Share—Share verses to study with your seekers that will help them be assured of the gift of eternal life. If they are already committed believers now, share eight weeks of Bible study in the areas of prayer, Bible reading, tithing, serving, and witnessing—to build healthy disciples.

Sail on Over to Day 6—Complete questions 7-9 of the review summary for day 6.

Charting My Course on Day 7—Based on today's reading, alter or add to your plan of action by charting your course on day 7.

Thought for the Day—Anyone who calls on God's name will find Him (Matt. 7:8).

DAY 4

Challenge Question—How long will sharing take?
Read—Isa. 52:7
Action Item—Define the term *salvation.*

How would you feel if you went to a party and your spouse told everyone he or she was single? Christians give many excuses for not telling others about Christ. We sometimes think we must be sophisticated and careful not to offend, but this can *leave the impression we serve other gods rather than our Savior.* Sometimes we bow for a long time to peer pressure, public opinion, and personal comfort rather than sharing the words that will bring others into the Kingdom. Rom. 10:9 reminds us to "confess with your mouth Jesus as Lord" (NASB). It is sometimes our own disobedience that keeps seekers from finding Christ.

Then again, often it is a seeker's own disobedience that keeps him or her from finding Christ. We are not accountable for the disobedience of others; we are only accountable for our own disobedience. People today are growing increasingly rebellious to God's laws. Christians may face long and hard times when witnessing to nonbelievers. It is important to remember the truths from Rom. 10:16-21: Not all people will seek Jesus. Not all people will want to hear about Jesus. Not all people will understand Jesus. And not all people will be transformed by Jesus, no matter how long and obedient we are as faithful servants. Remember, we are not accountable for the outcome, just the process of sharing.

We are to be like God relating to Israel; "All day long I held out my hands to a disobedient and obstinate people" (Rom. 10:21). Keep extending your hand.

Prayer—Confess any time when you have bowed to peer pressure, social concerns, or fear of offending and missed an opportunity to share Christ. Ask God to help you keep focused on His priorities, not those of the world.

Care—What steps of care are needed for you to speak to one of your seekers today?

Share—Share with your seekers your concern if they are delaying a response to the invitation of Jesus Christ. Be clear in letting them know you care about their eternal destiny.

Sail on Over to Day 6—Complete questions 10-12 of the review summary for day 6.

Charting My Course on Day 7—Based on today's reading, alter or add to your plan of action by charting your course on day 7.

Thought for the Day—Keep extending your hand.

DAY 5

Challenge Question—Where are your seekers now?
Read—Isa. 52:7-8
Action Item—Define what the outcome of faithful witnessing is.

If a city, building, or home is threatened, security guards or watchmen are sometimes put into place for protection. In our Bible passage for today the watchmen were awaiting the arrival of the messenger. Today the lost are awaiting the arrival of a messenger to help set them free from the bondage of sin. To be saved and sanctified for God's will and glory is the message. Both Jesus and we are the messengers. We are the watchmen awaiting the arrival of our King in the lives of those God has placed in our path.

A seeker's point of decision for Christ is a cause for rejoicing. The point where your seekers come full circle to lead others to your Savior is cause for jubilation. You may be squarely in the salvation decision-making mode with your seekers, or by evaluating Engel's Evangelistic Countdown you may determine that the process has stalled somewhere. Regardless of where your seekers are in their spiritual continuums, remain on guard and watch while your Master is at work in their lives. Keep vigilant and determine to retrace your witnessing steps as needed. You may even be saying: "I am still not ready to do this." Yet you must start somewhere and obey Christ's command regardless of how you feel.

Prayer—Ask God to help you keep a vigilant watch over your seekers. Ask Him to keep you posted on where they are on their spiritual journey, where you need to be silent in order to let Him work, and where you need to step in as His messenger.

Care—Care enough to share the words of the gospel with your seekers.

Share—Share enough to let your seekers know you care for them eternally.

Sail on Over to Day 6—Complete questions 13-15 of the review summary for day 6.

Charting My Course on Day 7—Based on today's reading, alter or add to your plan of action by charting your course on day 7.

Thought for the Day—"Therefore keep watch, because you do not know on what day your Lord will come" (Matt. 24:42).

DAY 6

Review Summary

Questions 1-15

1. What memory from your own spiritual journey has God shown you to employ with your seekers?

2. What characteristics of the one who originally shared Christ with you do you want to emulate?

3. Why do seekers give us a hard time before conversion? Why is perseverance essential to good spiritual parenting?

4. Why are there distractions when sharing the Good News?

5. How can you prepare for an attack when you're witnessing?

6. Why should you be grateful when the attack comes?

7. What part do you play in presenting the Good News?

8. What part does the Father, Son, and Holy Spirit play?

9. Why is basic Bible study important for the newly saved or unsaved?

10. What excuses have you given God for not sharing your precious Jesus?

11. What are two causes for people not coming to Christ?

12. How can you sensitively relate your concern for your seekers' spiritual condition?

14. Why is disciple-making important for your seeker?

13. Who are the watchmen in your life?

15. What is the outcome of faithful witnessing?

DAY 7

Charting My Course

Based on this week's readings, alter or add to your plan of action by charting your course.

	Name	Prayer Action	Care Action	Share Action	Prayer Answer
Day 1					
Day 2					
Day 3					
Day 4					
Day 5					
Day 6					
Day 7					

Week 12—A Multiplying Lighthouse

DAY 1

Challenge Question—Why should I share the plan of salvation?

Read—Acts 4:12-31

Action Item—Underline Acts 4:12.

The reason Christians must share the plan of salvation clearly, boldly, and often is that Jesus Christ is the only name under heaven in which people can find the peaceful, abundant lives they seek. Peter and John were not educated or trained in how to share the principles of salvation, but God gave them the confidence to do so in a way that caused all who heard them to marvel. Peter and John could not stop speaking the truth that sets men free (Acts 4:19-20). With every threat that they faced, God gave them increasing confidence and abundant grace. Likewise, we must present a clear, timely salvation message as followers of Christ.

Review the essential principles of sharing a clear salvation plan (see Appendix F, Gospel Outline). The principles of the love of God, our sinfulness, our separation from God, Christ's atoning death, and salvation by faith are the key elements to present to nonbelievers. The method, resource, or outline you use should contain these five fundamental biblical facts. Now would be a good time to review visual resources to help you offer a clear salvation plan. There are also many helpful tools in your Christian bookstore. Several are also listed in the Resource section of this book (Appendix J). Alternatively, you may choose to create your own diagram or outline. Whatever you choose, remember that a visual tool helps listeners stay focused and allows them to review your words after you have gone. As you practice sharing the plan of salvation with your accountability partner, you will begin to feel comfortable with the elements in your presentation. Between you and your accountability partner, prepare yourselves by asking each other salvation questions that may arise. Reminder: You are only accountable for sharing God's plan, not the hearer's decision.

Prayer—Share your heart with God, asking for understanding, clearness, and boldness in sharing the plan of salvation. Ask for His help in learning, focusing, and practicing the plan of salvation.

Care—Care enough about the spiritual condition of your seekers to practice the salvation plan this week to equip yourself to share the gospel with ease. Your seekers' lives depend upon the care and time you take.

Share—Practice sharing the plan of salvation using your visual tool of choice with your accountability partner. Practice until you both feel comfortable with your presentation.

Sail on Over to Day 6—Complete questions 1-3 of the review summary for day 6.

Charting My Course on Day 7—Based on today's reading, alter or add to your plan of action by charting your course on day 7.

Thought for the Day—"But Peter and John replied, 'Judge for yourselves whether it is right in God's sight to obey you rather than God. For we cannot help speaking about what we have seen and heard'" (Acts 4:19-20).

DAY 2

Challenge Question—How do I share the plan of salvation? (Part One)
Read—Acts 4:12-31
Action Item—Underline Acts 4:31.

When I share God's plan of the salvation I use eight simple steps with the *Four Spiritual Laws*. (See Gospel Outline, Appendix F.) First, I share a concise scripture-referenced personal testimony of my life before, during, and after accepting Christ as my Lord and Savior. Second, I ask the seekers if I may share a few Bible verses and tell how they changed my life. Third, I share the often-quoted John 3:16, stressing that it is a *fact* that God loves them and then I ask if they know this fact for certain. Fourth, I define sin as lawlessness, doubt, and rebellion against a holy God, citing Rom. 3:23. After I ask if they understand this definition and acknowledge that they have sinned against God, I quietly wait for them to reflect and answer. I tell them they do not have to share with me specific sins from their past, but that they simply need to acknowledge that they know at one or more points in their lives they have disobeyed what God has told them to do. Fifth, I share that despite their sin, God loves them and offers eternal life rather than the internal restless, unsettled, confusing, and uncertain lives they have been leading. I ask them if they can admit that their lives have been empty in some area, such as an absence of peace, joy, forgiveness, purposefulness, or the assurance that they are right with God.

Prayer—Ask God to help you learn the basic steps of His plan of salvation so you will always be ready to share when you encounter someone who needs to know.

Care—Carefully plan an outline for yourself using the eight suggested steps and scriptures to support each step. Place this outline in your Bible and learn it so you will be at ease and comfortable sharing with your seekers.

Share—Begin asking your seekers if you may share with them how your life changed when you understood God's plan of salvation. Use your outline, tract, or diagram to illustrate God's plan when sharing and to keep you focused and clear during your presentation. The fewer words you use the better. Let your seekers engage in the process by asking questions. If this is a one-sided conversation on your part, end your presentation and return to it at a later date.

Sail on Over to Day 6—Complete questions 4-6 of the review summary for day 6.

Charting My Course on Day 7—Based on today's reading, alter or add to your plan of action by charting your course on day 7.

Thought for the Day—The Lord is my light and my salvation.

DAY 3

Challenge Question—How do I share the plan of salvation?
(Part Two)

Read—Acts 4:31

Action Item—Define the term *boldness*.

The sixth step in sharing God's plan of salvation is to relate that just as in a job a person earns wages for working, that God tells us that the wages of sinfulness is death. Explain that spiritual death means separation from God spiritually, emotionally, physically, and eternally. Since God loves us He has provided a way to restore closeness with Him despite our past sin. Let them know that Jesus died for our sin and bore our deserved punishment. He was buried according to the Scriptures and rose on the third day. He shows us by the Holy Spirit, His life on earth, and Scripture how to live forever in right relationship to God.

Seventh, share that we can only receive this closeness to God through faith in the Lord Jesus Christ, "For it is by grace you have been saved, through faith—and this is not from yourselves, it is the gift of God—not by works, so that no one can boast" (Eph. 2:8-9). This is a free gift, and we choose either to accept it or reject it. If your seekers understand God's plan, invite them to accept this gift. Ask your seekers if they would like to accept Jesus as the Savior of their sins and make Him Lord over every area of their lives.

Step eight is to invite your seekers to pray a prayer of repentance (deep sorrow for sin), confessing their need of Christ and committing to follow Him as Lord and Savior. (See Appendix F for a detailed outline of God's plan of salvation and sample transitional sentences for each step.) If they accept your invitation to pray, invite them to repeat after you as you pray for their assurance of salvation, protection, strength, and the conservation of their decision. If they do not choose to pray right then, either ask them to contact you when they feel ready, or ask them again at another time. Stress, however, that now is the best time since they do not know if they will have another opportunity.

Prayer—Pray for God to give you a clear, bold, and timely opportunity to share His plan of salvation.

Care—Take as much time as needed to learn the eight basic steps of God's plan of salvation.

Share—Carefully describe the Four Spiritual Laws: (1) God's provision of purpose, peace, and life, (2) our choice of separation from God through our own attempts, (3) God's remedy through the Cross, and (4) our response to receive His free gift by faith and become God's eternal children.

Sail on Over to Day 6—Complete questions 7-9 of the review summary for day 6.

Chart My Course on Day 7—Based on today's reading, alter or add to your plan of action by charting your course on day 7.

Thought for the Day—"For it is by grace you have been saved, through faith—and this is not from yourselves, it is the gift of God—not by works, so that no one can boast" (Eph. 2:8-9).

DAY 4

Challenge Question—What is next?
Read—Acts 4:12
Action Item—Memorize Acts 4:12.

The Bible reminds us to consider carefully what is before us. It is very costly for nonbelievers to ignore the gospel we have set before them. Some may accept God's free gift, others will want to delay, while others will refuse it completely. As long as we have done our part to clearly, confidently, and consistently share God's gift, we are doing all that God desires and commands us to do. If a seeker has prayed the prayer of salvation with you, go on to the Basic Bible Studies follow-up stage (see Appendix G). If your seekers are hedging, continue to gently but firmly remind them that God has been waiting for them for a long time. While He watches over us and calls us by name, there is no assurance for any of us that there will be a tomorrow. Do not feel embarrassed or hesitant to make this clear. While we do not want to present unhealthy fear, healthy fear of God is good. Let the Holy Spirit prompt you on how much to emphasize God's providential grace. If your seekers refuse to accept God's gift of salvation, ask if you may continue to pray for them and maybe discuss spiritual issues with them at a later time. Then keep on praying.

Prayer—Ask God to give you His peace in doing your part of sharing the gospel. Confess to Him if you have fallen short, and thank Him for doing His part.

Care—Assess the spiritual choices being made by each of your seekers.

Share—Continue to look for the open doors God gives to share the words of the gospel with each person on your prayer list.

Sail on Over to Day 6—Complete questions 10-12 of the review summary for day 6.

Charting My Course on Day 7—Based on today's reading, alter or add to your plan of action by charting your course on day 7.

Thought for the Day—Let the Holy Spirit prompt you as you share the story of God's grace.

DAY 5

Challenge Question—Where are your seekers now?
Read—Acts 16:31

The Bible tells of a guard who pleaded with Paul and Silas for his salvation and the salvation of his family. Paul responded, "Believe in the Lord Jesus, and you will be saved—you and your household" (Acts 16:31). The guard went home, told his family about Jesus, and they were saved. My family did not all trust Christ the same time I did. Yet I did not stop praying for them to come to accept God's plan for them. Do not give up on your seekers now.

Have faith in God that someday they will believe. For some seekers to believe you will need to retrace the 90-Day *Lighting the Way* journey. If your seekers have accepted Christ, continue on with 8 or 10 basic Bible study sessions to allow them to ask you spiritual questions, to help them learn more about how to use the Bible, to demonstrate an obedient walk in Christ now that they can truly understand it, and to ensure their spiritual growth and sustained commitment. (See Basic Bible Studies, Appendix G.)

It is important now for you to celebrate the steps you have taken through *Lighting the Way* that have guided you into greater obedience as a follower of Jesus Christ. You need never return to the "witnessing guilt" stage again, because you have learned and applied Prayer, Care, and Share principles. Dr. H. B. London from Focus on the Family once said, "What we do upon any great occasion (like sharing our faith), depends on what we already are . . . and what we are will be the result of previous years of self-discipline." Evaluate the spiritual growth of your seekers, but maintain your own growth in sharing your faith and enjoy the blessings that come from your obedience to God. Our witness to His great love is to be a reminder of God's covenant work of redemption to all who will see and hear.

Prayer—Confess any doubt you may have had in believing your seekers would be saved.

Care—Carefully evaluate the progress of your seekers using Engel's Evangelistic Countdown.

Share—Share with your accountability partner the spiritual growth progress of your seekers and how you have grown in sharing your faith since you first began *Lighting the Way.*

Sail on Over to Day 6—Complete questions 13-15 of the review summary for day 6.

Chart My Course on Day 7—Based on today's reading, alter or add to your plan of action by charting your course on day 7.

Thought for the Day—Our witness to His great love is to be a reminder of God's covenant work of redemption to all who will see and hear.

DAY 6

Review Summary

Questions 1-15

1. Why must Christians share God's plan of salvation?

2. Why did Peter and John have confidence to share God's gift of eternal life?

3. Why do we need to practice sharing the plan of salvation?

4. Can you describe the first five steps in God's plan of salvation?

5. Why is using scripture important in sharing God's plan of salvation?

6. Why are the fewer words you use in sharing salvation better than a lot of words?

7. What benefits can you convey to your seekers that a child of God has after accepting Christ into every area of his or her life?

8. Why is explaining that Jesus lived, died, and rose from the dead important to God's plan?

9. What makes God's plan through Jesus different from what other teachers, prophets, or spiritual leaders offer? (Hint: where are these other leaders now?)

10. What are some of the costs that seekers might pay if they do not accept Christ today?

11. What else does God want you to do about the spiritual condition of your seekers?

12. What is the next step for you if one of your seekers prays for salvation?

13. How can you increase your faith so that your family and unsaved friends will see Christ in you?

14. Why are basic Bible studies important to new converts?

15. How can a lifestyle of using Prayer, Care, and Share principles bring blessing to your family and to you?

DAY 7

Charting My Course

Based on this week's readings, alter or add to your plan of action by charting your course.

	Name	Prayer Action	Care Action	Share Action	Prayer Answer
Day 1					
Day 2					
Day 3					
Day 4					
Day 5					
Day 6					
Day 7					

Week 13—A Lifestyle Lighthouse

DAY 1

Challenge Question—Is my Lighthouse making a difference?

Read—Isa. 40:31

Action Item—List the benefits of waiting upon God as His witnesses.

Someone once said to me, "Now what do I do? I shared the plan of salvation with my brother; He tells me he will *think* about it." I told him to respond to his brother by saying, "You remind me of the person whose car stalled on the railway of an oncoming train. She had to *think* about jumping and saving her life or trying to get her car started. Sadly, she chose the latter and died." Your seekers need to know that the moment of death is uncertain for each of us and that they are already in the line of an oncoming train. Eternity is facing the nonbelievers God has placed in your path. As you share the good news of Jesus Christ, it will make an eternal difference in their lives, in their families, in their cities, in their nation, and in the world.

Second Thess. 2:13 says we should be thankful for our salvation and sanctification in Christ. Our thank-You to God comes in the form of being obedient disciples, even in areas where we may struggle. We will reflect the depth of our gratitude for being saved in our obedient witness to the unsaved. If we wait upon the Spirit of God as we witness, He will take away our fear and our personal doubt or concern over rejection. Remember, it was only when Peter looked at the waves instead of Jesus that he started to sink. Waiting and walking with God will give you freedom and power to help rescue the lost. Ps. 138:3 says: "When I called, you answered me; you made me bold and stouthearted." Be a bold and stouthearted Lighthouse to make a difference in your world.

Prayer—Confess any time when you have not been appropriately bold in conveying the need for urgency to a seeker accepting Christ as Lord and Savior.

Care—What steps do you need to take to exercise a meaningful act of kindness for your seekers this week. Choose an act that will assure them of your abiding love regardless of their spiritual decisions.

Share—Continue to walk and talk your faith with your seekers.

Sail on Over to Day 6—Complete questions 1-3 of the review summary for day 6.

Charting My Course on Day 7—Based on today's reading, alter or add to your plan of action by charting your course on day 7.

Thought for the Day—"When I called, you answered me; you made me bold and stouthearted" (Ps. 138:3).

DAY 2

Challenge Question—How can I help make lasting disciples?
Read—Isa. 40:31
Action Item—Identify the four benefits of waiting on God.

Within the first 24 hours after conversion, new Christians need to embark upon at least eight weeks of Bible study with a mature believer. The basics of how to walk with Christ are foundational to building lasting and multiplying disciples. After Pentecost Christians "were continually devoting themselves to the apostles' teaching and to fellowship, to the breaking of bread and to prayer" (Acts 2:42, NASB). New believers today need the same intense fellowship, Bible study, communion, prayer, and witnessing disciplines as converts in the Early Church. Incorporating these new lifestyle priorities takes time.

Usually new converts will enthusiastically join you in weekly studies with great relish. About six weeks into the routine, however, they may find excuses and begin to miss meetings. This behavior is not unusual because the devil is still fighting the converts. We must explain that these excuses are a retreat back into their behavior prior to conversion. The devil is battling to pull them away from basic disciplines of faith.

Be firm with new converts and remind them that God is aware of their priorities. Be prepared to pray with new converts to find victory over any area of rebellion. If necessary help them confess sin, start again, and exercise walking in the Holy Spirit-led life that God desires. It is also important that seekers see you keeping your appointments with them. New converts are vulnerable to tremendous attacks. Learning the basics of a strong faith walk will give them the defenses they need for a lifetime of Christian service and victory. (See Basic Bible Studies, Appendix G.)

Prayer—Pray regularly and often for the protection of your seekers' new lives in Christ. Pray also that they will be strengthened and firmly grounded in spiritual discipline.

Care—Find a picture of Jesus tending lambs to give to your new converts. Remind them that God is helping them each day as they mature spiritually.

Share—Remind your new converts that the devil is seeking to destroy what God has done and is doing in their lives. Remind them to pray for God to protect and defend them against these attacks. Help them confess and start again when necessary.

Sail on Over to Day 6—Complete questions 4-6 of the review summary for day 6.

Charting My Course on Day 7—Based on today's reading, alter or add to your plan of action by charting your course on day 7.

Thought for the Day—The basics of how to walk with Christ are foundational to building lasting and multiplying disciples.

DAY 3

Challenge Question—Why is my commitment to spiritual disciplines important?

Read—Isa. 40:31

Action Item—Recite Isa. 40:31.

When Jesus commanded in John 21:17 "Tend My sheep" (NASB), He knew there would be many lost lambs in our path who are easily frightened, directionless, and unclean. We, too, were like these lost sheep who had gone astray. Jesus was the answer to our fear, failure, and lack of direction. If there was not a mature believer to pray for you and care for your spiritual concerns when you were first saved, you know firsthand how difficult this journey was.

The people who shared Christ with me until my salvation quickly dropped out of my life. I was left alone to discover for myself just how I was to work out this new life so different from my past. My commitment was deep, genuine, and unwavering. I started leading a Bible study in my home within the first six weeks of my conversion just so I could learn spiritual discipline. Early on I instinctively knew I needed to take a few others along with me on the journey.

Having regular Bible studies with new converts is such a true joy. Such precious "babies" deserve a great deal of attention. Give new converts plenty of encouragement in each new step they take. Find ways to reward their progress. You might even give them a certificate when they have completed the first eight weeks of Bible study. (See Basic Bible Studies, Appendix G.)

Prayer—Ask God to help you plan and stay committed to your weekly schedule by giving 30 to 60 minutes a week faithfully to your new converts.

Care—Plan a short Bible study on one of the basics of discipleship. Take great care to keep the study short. Do not overwhelm converts with too much too soon.

Share—Tell your new converts that you are available at any time to answer questions that may arise. Give them a short devotional to do each day. Write a note reminding them of the benefits of starting each day with prayer and a scripture verse. Write your name and the date of their conversion on the inside cover of the Bible study.

Sail on Over to Day 6—Complete questions 7-9 of the review summary for day 6.

Charting My Course on Day 7—Based on today's reading, alter or add to your plan of action by charting your course on day 7.

Thought for the Day—Give new converts plenty of encouragement in each new step they take.

DAY 4

Challenge Question—Am I in a battle too?
Read—Isa. 40:31
Action Item—Memorize Isa. 40:31.

"Let us not become weary in doing good, for at the proper time we will reap" (Gal. 6:9). These words ring true as we endeavor to be faithfully committed disciples of our new converts. Without the strength of the Lord we may feel tempted to give up, or we may stop trying to be patient as our new converts begin growing spiritually. The New Testament speaks of love, nourishment, protection, and training for new converts. Spiritual parents of new converts must model the love of Christ to them. They must help converts learn the Word of God in such a way that each day their walk with God will be strengthened and prepared for His service. Spiritual parents must teach converts some defense against the devil, who is seeking to destroy, divert, and distract them. Here are 10 basics in follow-up that are essential (*Conserve the Converts*, 88).

1. Stay on the subject without digressing into your personal feelings.
2. Be selective with questions so you do not impose on their time.
3. Teach slowly. New converts are just spiritual babies.
4. Give them small amounts at a time.
5. Stick to the basics without digressing into controversial issues.
6. Know the lesson and be prepared.
7. Beware of your approach, making sure neither your language nor your physical presence is offensive.
8. Be positive.
9. Teach as a learner, not one with all the answers.
10. Make your points without arguing.

Prayer—Ask God to help you be positive and teachable in discipling new converts.

Care—Carefully review this study for guidelines in teaching new converts. Consider purchasing resources for following up with new converts. (See Resources, Appendix J.)

Share—Share the basics of a strong faith walk with your new converts in simple Bible studies for 8 to 10 weeks. Help them get into a church Sunday School class or Bible study to keep them growing. (Note: this does not have to be your church, but one where Christ is preached and lifted up as the one and only way to be saved and sanctified for eternal life, service, and expansion.)

Sail on Over to Day 6—Complete questions 10-12 of the review summary for day 6.

Charting My Course on Day 7—Based on today's reading, alter or add to your plan of action by charting your course on day 7.

Thought for the Day—"Let us not become weary in doing good, for at the proper time we will reap" (Gal. 6:9).

DAY 5

Challenge Question—What is next?
Reread—Isa. 40:31

From time to time, we all get weary in doing good. We may even question whether our Lighthouse lifestyle of prayer, care, and share is effective. Yet when we experience the exhilaration that comes from obeying God as His Spirit prompts us, it gives us renewed energy and a reminder of His faithfulness. This inspires us to step out in faith even further. God does not expect that new converts will be mature disciple-makers, just as He does not expect them to be mature disciples on the first day. He is pleased with our continued growth in witnessing.

I remember thinking I had to have lots of salvation verses memorized before I could witness. Then I learned about the simple effectiveness of using a tract. I got so excited over the results of presenting the gospel with the tract that it inspired me to learn the verses one by one over time. Just as in any area of our walk with God, there is a point where we make a radical change to be obedient. Then God continues to lead us in these areas and refines our obedience.

You have committed every day for three months to give your witnessing skills a jump-start. *Lighting the Way* is only the beginning of a rewarding walk with God in sharing your faith. Being a light to this and succeeding generations is a privilege you do not want to miss. God will not neglect new spiritual babies or obedient disciples. Lay up treasures of saved souls in heaven by your effective witness. Let His light shine from your Lighthouse. Your reward will come the day you hear "well done, good and faithful servant!" (Matt. 25:21).

Prayer—Ask God to give you new strength each day to serve Him and glorify Him by your witness in prayer, caring, and sharing the Good News!

Care—As God leads, continue to demonstrate His love through action with those who have not yet discovered His eternal gift.

Share—Continue to exercise those principles of prayer, caring, and sharing that will give you a lifetime of joy as multitudes also find the Light of Life for themselves.

Sail on Over to Day 6—Complete questions 13-15 of the review summary for day 6.

Charting My Course on Day 7—List the names of others God is placing on your heart for salvation.

Thought for the Day—Being a light to this and succeeding generations is a privilege you do not want to miss. Let His light shine from your Lighthouse.

DAY 6

Review Summary

Questions 1-15

1. Why is sharing about spiritual eternity an urgent matter?

2. What will we do if we are thankful for our own salvation?

3. What does God promise if we call upon Him?

4. What are the four benefits of waiting on God as His watchmen and messenger?

5. Why do you think the first 24 hours are so critical to new converts?

6. What often makes new converts drop their commitment to Bible study?

7. Why are 8 to 10 weeks of basic Bible study important for new converts?

8. Why should the studies be kept short?

9. Why is sharing the gospel without follow-up spiritually irresponsible?

10. How are you also in the spiritual battle along with your new converts?

11. What are the four things new converts must have?

12. Why are the suggestions for how to lead new converts in basic Bible study important?

13. What will God do if we become weary in doing good?

14. Who has God placed in your path that will cause you to revisit the *Lighting the Way* journey?

15. How can you thank your accountability partner for his or her faithfulness to your spiritual growth in effectively sharing your faith?

DAY 7

Charting My Course

List the names of others God is placing on your heart for salvation.

	Name	Prayer Action	Care Action	Share Action	Prayer Answer
Day 1					
Day 2					
Day 3					
Day 4					
Day 5					
Day 6					
Day 7					

Appendixes

APPENDIX A

Prayer List
(Random Selection Ideas)

"In all your ways acknowledge him, and he will make your paths straight" (Prov. 3:6).

"The prayer of a righteous man is powerful and effective" (James 5:16).

Thank God for the one who brought the gospel to you.

- Ask God to search your life for any disobedience in your witnessing to others.
- Ask Him to give you compassion for the lost.
- Ask God to help you see the spiritual needs of others.
- Confess any time you neglected to pray because it was time-consuming or inconvenient.
- Ask God to make you a "model of prayer."
- Ask God to confirm that the three to five people on your 90-day list are the right ones to whom you should be actively witnessing.
- Petition God to make you sensitive enough to see the difference between spiritual needs and problems.
- Thank God for the fullness of joy He has given you.
- Ask God to help you know what is His part and what is your part in witnessing to others.
- Thank God for the accountability partner He has given you.
- Ask the Holy Spirit to fill your heart with confidence, boldness, and perseverance.
- Confess any ways you have hindered someone's prayers for the lost.
- Pray for God to make His joy powerfully known in the lives of your seekers.
- Use all the scriptures from Week 3, Day 1 and pray for each of your seekers.

- Pray for God to help you see where and when to biblically defend moral standards.
- Ask God to show you clearly where your seekers are on Engel's Evangelistic Countdown.
- Confess any times when you have quenched the Holy Spirit's prompting for prayer for the lost.
- Ask God to take away any nervousness you may feel that keeps you from witnessing.
- Confess any area of your prayer life that is not pleasing to God. Ask Him to protect your devotional time.
- Ask God to take the spiritual blinders off your seekers.
- Pray that God will help you bring out the best in others.
- Ask God to give you boldness to witness in words and deeds.
- Pray that God will help you use one of your frailties for His glory in witnessing to your seekers.
- Pray that God will help you overcome fear when sharing with family members.
- Ask God to give you His courage at times when others would pull away from your seekers.
- Place a card with Rom. 12:12 on your refrigerator to remind you how to pray for seekers.
- Pray for the Holy Spirit to work in the lives of your seekers before you go to witness.
- In your prayers to God, always remember to name both your seekers and their prayer requests.
- Pray for the compassion to see your lost friends as God sees them.
- Ask God to show you what holiness means (see Sanctification resources in Appendix J).
- Ask God to bless those who persecute you.
- Pray for other Lighthouses in your neighborhood.

- Thank God that His Word cuts to the heart of seekers and never returns void.
- Thank God for the many gifts He has given you.
- Pray for God to show you the gifts He has given your seekers.
- Pray for your seekers on your prayer list as you pass by their homes.
- Pray with your eyes open.
- Ask God to release His power and grace in the lives of the unsaved.
- Pray without ceasing.
- Ask God to give your seekers a thirst for His Word.
- Pray for the Lord to give you wisdom to understand your seekers.
- Thank God He has been with you during rough times.
- Ask God to bring helpful verses to your mind.
- Ask God to show you what gifts He has given you, and express your gratitude for them.
- Pray that your good works would be evident to seekers.
- Ask God to help you learn witnessing skills.
- Pray for the Holy Spirit to make your seekers sensitive to your words before each step.
- Pray for God to help you witness in spontaneous situations.
- Ask God to help you offer hope to your seekers by meeting their special needs.
- Pray for an opportunity to use one of your witnessing tools.
- Ask God to keep you a strong witness like those of the Early Church.
- Pray for wisdom in forming your personal testimony.

- Confess to God that you are not always patient. Ask Him for help being patient with your seekers.
- Ask God to mold you into a good witness to those whose lives are different from yours.
- Ask God to remind you what you were like before accepting Him.
- Pray for a bold, clear personal testimony and the receptivity of your seekers' hearts to it.
- Ask God to help you do your part witnessing for Him, and thank Him for doing His part.
- Confess any time when you should have shared God's love but bowed to peer pressure or social concerns instead.
- Ask God to help you be a vigilant "shepherd" over your seekers.
- Ask God to help you as you practice telling others of His plan of salvation.
- Pray for a clear opportunity to share God's plan of salvation.
- Confess where you have fallen short of God's will in sharing His love.
- Confess any doubt or impatience you may have over your seekers' day of salvation.
- Pray for God to show you how to appropriately express the urgency of salvation.
- Pray for God to protect, strengthen, and ground new converts into disciples.
- Pray for God to help you in your commitment to having short, regular, follow-up Bible studies.
- Ask God to keep you teachable so that others may learn from you.
- Ask God to help you be an effective praying, caring, and sharing Lighthouse.

APPENDIX B

Care List
(Random Selection Ideas)

"It is more blessed to give than to receive" (Acts 20:35).

Commit to carefully completing each of the 90 days in *Lighting the Way*.

- Offer to do some mending for a working mom.
- Find a newspaper or magazine article that would interest one of your seekers.
- Take a bag of groceries to an unemployed family.
- Do a lot of listening, not talking.
- Take seekers to church or other gatherings where the gospel is clearly presented.
- Have lots of Christian greeting cards on hand to send at special times.
- Look up Phil. 4:19 and have it ready to present to a special seeker with a special need.
- Invite seekers to holiday gatherings, and during mealtime share that for which you are thankful.
- Give your seeker a devotional book, Bible, Christian video, or CD.
- Look to make a daring act of kindness that will only be possible with God's help.
- Write out prayer requests to God for your seekers and mail it to each of them.
- Offer to fix a seeker's car.
- Take a favorite hymn or poem about a holiday to family gatherings.
- Invite seekers to your home to see what a godly family is like.
- Introduce yourself to another Christian your seekers may know.
- Demonstrate care for others by leading a godly life worthy of the seekers' modeling.
- Look for one wholesome trait in each seeker.
- Make a "Walk Date" with a seeker this week.
- Give your seekers a Bible or resource with key verses underlined.
- Provide a recreational outing for a single parent on a tight budget.
- Look for ways to help your seekers see that God's security is the only true security.
- Provide relief to a seeker with an elderly parent by helping with care-taking tasks.
- Locate a reputable house-cleaning service for a working neighbor.
- Deliver cookies for no special occasion.
- Invite a seeker to your home for a barbecue.
- Volunteer to watch a seeker's house and pets while he or she is away.
- Give a hug.
- Give a seeker an affirming comment.
- Drop off a meal when illness strikes.
- Read a story to a youngster.
- Offer to pick up kids from school during emergencies.
- Take a walk with your neighbor.
- Provide a ride to a church event.
- Share a meal with a seeker during busy holidays.
- Drive someone to a doctor appointment.
- Assist someone during a move.
- Send a Christian greeting card with a gift certificate in an area of interest to your seeker.
- Honor a seeker with a public radio greeting.
- Bake a cake for a seeker's birthday.
- Deliver some of your garden flowers or produce to your seekers.
- Shovel snow, rake leaves, or help mow a yard.
- Go Christmas caroling while delivering cookies.
- Take photos of your seekers' children on special occasions.
- Cut out news/magazine articles on subjects your seekers are interested in.

- Attend a seeker's child's school activity if the seeker is unable to go.
- Offer to help a seeker with a difficult household task.
- Place key Bible verses in your Bible for quick reference.
- Receive a seeker's gifts to you with gratitude, a thank-you note, and a hug.
- Give used toys and clothes to meet your seekers' needs when appropriate.
- Introduce seekers to your Christian friends who have a spiritual background similar to theirs.
- Include seekers in your holiday plans.
- Acquire Christian sympathy cards on job loss, bereavement, or fear to have ready when your seekers need them.
- Highlight salvation verses in your Bible or tab them for easy access.
- Discover your spiritual gifts and use them with your seekers.
- Encourage seekers to express their shortcomings when they hear you express yours.
- Assemble your gospel presentation tools with care.
- Carefully take time to form your personal testimony.
- Share an ethnic meal with your seekers.
- Set up a basic Bible study group.
- Share the plan of salvation.
- Place a salvation outline in your Bible along with other helpful tools.
- Practice the eight steps to effectively presenting the Four Spiritual Laws.
- Carefully evaluate the spiritual progress of each of your seekers.
- Find a lighthouse picture to give new converts as a way of telling then about the light of Jesus.
- Carefully plan and prepare for basic Bible study follow-up meetings.

APPENDIX C

Share List
(Sequential Selection Ideas)

"Give the reason for the hope that you have" (1 Pet. 3:15).

- Share with a believing friend how you have committed to the *Lighting the Way* journey.
- Share with God where you have let some prayer, care, share area slide.
- Ask one person where he or she is spiritually and just listen.
- Share the names of three to five seekers with your accountability partner for his or her prayer list.
- Ask your partner to pray that your "care action" would root deeply into seekers' hearts.
- Tell your unsaved friend it is Jesus who teaches you how to meet needs and be thoughtful.
- Tell a seeker one wholesome trait he or she has for which you are grateful to God.
- Share with your prayer partner how you moved through Engel's Evangelistic Countdown.
- Share one area where you have turned a personal disappointment into God's "appointment" for witnessing.
- Ask your seekers if they see God's love, joy, and kindness in you, and listen to their responses.
- Look for a way to share God's moral standard in a confused world this week.
- Ask each seeker for a specific prayer request.
- Ask seekers how their prayers are being answered, and rejoice with them.
- Tell each seeker how privileged you are to be able to pray for him or her.
- As answers to prayer unfold, remember to share with your seekers it is God who is answering.
- Ask your seekers how they are seeing God at work in their lives.
- Share with your prayer partner how you are growing in your witnessing obedience.
- Show forgiveness in order to teach forgiveness.
- Ask your seekers how they most appreciate receiving love: affection, acts of service, verbal affirmation, etc.
- Tell your seekers being a good person is not enough to get them to heaven because we will always fall short.
- Request that your seekers read some key verses of Scripture along with you.
- Share any of your own past failures with your seekers to set the tone for their confession.
- Share with your seekers what the word *redemption* means to you. Use specific examples.
- Show your seekers how to find difficult Bible references (i.e., John vs. 1 John).
- Send a note with a meaningful scripture to your seekers.
- Look for ways to encourage seekers by highlighting the gifts God has given them.
- Remind seekers you are still being transformed, and God is not finished with you yet.
- Encourage seekers when they start using the "words" of faith in conversation.
- Share how hope is more than wishful thinking.
- Look for ways to talk about your "Great Christ" rather than your "good day."
- Discuss the difference between healthy fear and unhealthy fear with your seekers.
- Practice sharing your personal testimony with friends.
- Direct seekers to Internet evangelism sites.
- Give your seekers a *JESUS* video for adults or children and then discuss it with them later.
- Learn encouraging words in your seekers' language if different from yours.
- Practice sharing a well-designed gospel tract with a family member.
- Share God's plan of salvation with your seekers.

- Review the Four Spiritual Laws with each seeker on your prayer list. (See Appendix F.)
- Share a short devotional gift designed for new converts.
- Share a small New Testament with your seekers (see Resources, Appendix J).
- Begin an 8- to 10-week Bible study whether or not your seeker has accepted Jesus.
- Help new converts find a church that fits their needs.
- Help new converts get involved in a new church by going with them for a few weeks.
- Continue to faithfully exercise the prayer, care, and share principles.

APPENDIX D

When Additional Help Is Needed

- **I am trying to get through on good works.**
  Luke 16:15; Acts 13:38-39; Rom. 3:20; 10:3; Gal. 2:16; Eph. 2:8-9

- **I lack faith.**
  Rom. 10:17; Phil. 4:9; Heb. 10:23; 1 John 5:11-13

- **To show God's willingness to forgive.**
  Ps. 86:5; John 6:37; 1 Thess. 5:24; Heb. 10:23

- **I feel that God cannot forgive me.**
  Pss. 86:5; 103:12; Isa. 1:18; 43:25; Matt. 12:31; 1 John 1:9

- **I am afraid that I will not be able to hold out.**
  Matt. 11:28-30; Rom. 14:4; Gal. 2:20; Phil. 1:6; 4:13; 1 Pet. 1:5; Jude 24

- **The Christian life is too hard.**
  Ps. 37:23-24; Prov. 13:15; Isa. 41:10; Matt. 11:28-30; 1 Cor. 10:13; Gal 2:20; Phil. 4:13

- **I just don't feel like I've been saved.**
  Rom. 5:1; 10:9-10; Eph. 2:8-9; James 1:21; 1 Pet. 1:23; 1 John 5:10-13; Rev. 3:20

- **I'm not ready yet.**
  Prov. 27:1; Rom. 9:20; 2 Cor. 6:2; Heb. 2:3; 3:7-9; James 4:13-14

- **I am lukewarm spiritually.**
  Matt. 7:21; Rev. 2:1-5; 3:14-21

- **I have trouble forgiving someone.**
  Matt. 6:14-15; 18:21-35; Mark 11:25-26; Luke 6:37

- **I cling to an old profession.**
  Matt. 7:21-23; Heb. 5:9; Rev. 2:1-5; 3:14-21

- **I am a Roman Catholic.**
  Matt. 23:9; Mark 3:31-35; John 14:6; 1 Tim. 2:5; Heb. 7:23-25; 10:11-14

- **I am holding back.**
  Luke 9:62; Heb. 2:3; 3:7-9; 10:38-39

- **I believe in spiritism.**
  Lev. 20:6; John 14:6; Gal. 5:19-21; 1 John 4:1-3; Rev. 21:8

- **I am afraid I will lose my job.**
  Pss. 1; 37:25; 75:6-7; 84:11; Matt. 6:33; Mark 8:36-37

- **I am too great a sinner.**
  Pss. 86:5; 103:12; Isa. 1:18; 43:25; 55:7; Luke 18:9-14; John 6:37

- **I cannot accept the Bible.**
  2 Tim. 3:16-17; 1 Pet. 1:25; 2 Pet. 1:20-21; Rev. 22:18-19

- **I fear ridicule.**
  Luke 12:4-5

- **I cannot give up ____ in my life.**
  Gal. 5:19-21

- **I only see hypocrites.**
  Rom. 14:13

- **I cannot forgive.**
  Matt. 6:15; Phil. 4:13

- **I am in grief.**
  Matt. 5:4

- **I need guidance.**
  Prov. 3:5-6

- **I need peace.**
  John 14:27

- **I am tempted.**
  1 Cor. 10:13

- **I am weary.**
  1 Pet. 5:6-7

APPENDIX E

Personal Testimony Work Sheet

Your personal testimony should be short, concise, and simple. Because this is *your* testimony, others will not disagree with your experience. It should create an interest in your hearers to hear more about Christ. A good scriptural model to review would be Acts 26:4-23. At first use another piece of paper and list ideas or thoughts that illustrate each section in the outline. Think of one central theme such as lack of peace, joy, direction, purpose, guilt, bitterness, or anger. Repeat that theme in all sections. Write out each section and share it with your accountability partner for clarity. Revise and practice, using a timer, to develop a three- to five-minute version. Avoid using words that are unfamiliar and confusing to nonbelievers, such as *denomination, salvation, grace,* or *regeneration.*

SECTION I

Opening Question to Get Attention of Audience (Use your central theme to form this question.)

_____

_____

SECTION II

Before I Decided to Follow Christ (Share a negative attitude, emotion, or behavior along with a simple example of how this affected your life and choices. Include some of your positive attitudes, beliefs, and convictions to give balance and accuracy. Share how your positive traits were not enough to offset the negative ones. Conclude this section using your central theme in one sentence.)

_____

_____

_____

SECTION III

When I Decided to Follow Christ (Share the Four Spiritual Laws in brief detail yet in a conversational way. To personalize your testimony, you might use the name of the one who shared the gospel steps with you. Saying this person's name aloud will give you confidence and bring you a spirit of genuine thankfulness that will be evident. Use the scripture verse that brought you to a change of heart, mind, or will. Conclude the final sentence using your central theme and your recognition of spiritual need.)

_____

_____

_____

_____

_____

SECTION IV

Since I Decided to Follow Christ (Share positive emotions, attitudes, or behaviors as opposites to those described in Section I. Give one example to illustrate the effect Jesus has had on you. For example, *I desire to read the Bible more* or *God has helped me break a habit of being critical.* Be sure to use your central theme in the concluding sentence and restate your scripture verse).

_____

_____

_____

_____

SECTION V

Concluding Statement (State that since Christ has made such a difference in your life you would like to have the opportunity to share how your seekers might come to trust and follow Him too. For example, as you repeat your scripture verse ask if they have ever thought about knowing Jesus Christ in a personal way, or if they have ever thought of what it means to have Him as Lord of their lives. Assess their responses, and either ask for an appointment at a later time or go

to the Gospel Outline [Appendix F] and share
the salvation steps.)

_____

_____

_____

_____

_____

APPENDIX F

Gospel Outline and Transitional Sentences

STEP 1: Share a short, concise, Scripture-based personal testimony of your life before, when, and after you decided to follow Jesus Christ.

STEP 2: Ask the seeker if you may share a few Bible verses that have changed your life.

STEP 3: Quote John 3:16 and achieve common ground by asking if your seekers have ever heard it before. Most people have heard John 3:16, and finding this common ground makes them feel less ignorant. Ask your seekers if they know for certain by this verse that God loves them. If they say they do, ask them how they know. If they say they do not know, ask them if you can share how they can know. Either way you are diagnosing their spiritual condition.

STEP 4: Define sin (willfull disobedience to God). Remind the seekers that all of us have fallen short of what God intended for us. Showing Rom. 3:23, share one example of how you fell short of God's glory before coming to trust Jesus Christ.

Create an "atmosphere" of vulnerability to God's plan by showing your own vulnerability. Ask if they understand the definition of sin in the Bible. Ask if they have ever sinned according to this definition. (You may have to ask this several ways because they will hedge, rationalize away, or discount their sinfulness.) Quietly allow any silence to be deafening by letting it linger. Allow the Holy Spirit time to bring some specific sin to your seekers' minds. Share with them that they need not share the specifics of their sin, they only need to acknowledge in some way that they have committed sin by disobeying what they knew God did or did not want in their lives.

STEP 5: Share that despite their sins, God loves them and has been waiting a long time for them to receive His gift of peace, joy, and eternal, purposeful life. Ask if they are tired of their internal restlessness, feeling unsettled, confused, and uncertain about life. Ask if they can admit that their life has been empty, or if they have been unable to change a bad habit. Ask if they have assurance they are spiritually right with God.

STEP 6: Share that without a right relationship with God our lives are very distant from Him, so distant that we do not even know who He is. Help them know that this great distance causes ongoing sin, resulting in further distance and lack of peace. Share with them that this spiritual separation causes us to constantly feel unsettled physically, emotionally, intellectually. Your seekers may never have realized any connection before, so explain how lack of peace affects every area of our lives. Explain the Four Spiritual Laws:

Law 1   God loves us and wants to be close to us. Jesus died for our sins, offering us His peace, purpose, and love (John 3:16).

Law 2   Humans are sinful and separated from a holy God. Jesus paid the price for our sinfulness while we were in sin (Prov. 14:12; Rom. 6:23).

Law 3   God provided a way to close the gap. Jesus died on the Cross and rose on the third day, paying the penalty of our sin and showing us how to have a relationship with God (1 Pet. 3:18).

Law 4   We must be sorry for sinning against God, confess our sin, turn away from sinfulness, and follow God to be right with Him. Jesus forgives our sin if we confess our sin, turn from our sin, and follow Him as Lord and Savior (Rom. 10:9; Rev. 3:20).

STEP 7: Share what seekers must do for salvation.

1. Admit their need of God and feel genuine sorrow for sin.
2. Be willing to turn away from sin and turn toward God (1 John 1:9).

3. Believe by faith that Jesus, God's Son, died on the Cross, rose from the grave, and offers forgiveness of sin (Eph. 2:8-9).

4. Invite Jesus Christ to come into their lives and control their lives through the Holy Spirit (Rev. 3:20).

STEP 8: If they desire, lead the seekers in an invitation prayer.

Dear Jesus: I know that I have sinned against You. I am deeply sorry for sinning against You. I need Your forgiveness. I believe You died for my sin. I am willing to turn from sin and follow You for the rest of my life. I ask You to come into my life and show me how to live in a way that is pleasing to You. I want to trust and follow You as Lord and Savior of my life.

(Read Rom. 10:13 to the seeker. Rejoice, pray, and start them in basic Bible study [see Appendix G and "Follow-up of New Converts" in Appendix J, Resources].)

APPENDIX G

Basic Bible Studies for New and Growing Christians

This is an example of what a basic Bible study for new believers looks like. See Appendix J, Basic Bible Studies, for this particular study.

Lesson 1

Christians Belong to God

Name: _____

Memory Verse: *Here I [Jesus] am! I stand at the door and knock. If anyone hears My voice and opens the door, I will come in.* (Revelation 3:20, TEB)

Find the Bible verses in these lessons in your Bible. Or, find them in your New Testament. John 1:12 means the Book of John, chapter 1, verse 12. Find the list of books at the beginning of your Bible. You will find the page numbers for all the books. Turn to the page numbers where the books start. Find the Bible verses and read them. Then read each sentence and question in the lessons. Write the answers in your own words. Or, use the words from the Bible. (The verses from the Old Testament are printed for you.)

1. Read John 1:12. I have received Jesus *into my heart.* I believe Jesus Christ is God. Now, I am one of His _____. Jesus is my *Savior.* I am a *Christian.*

2. Jesus is a Friend to all people who receive Him. Jesus wants to come *into our hearts.* He is waiting to come. But, we must ask Him to come. Read Revelation 3:20 and answer the questions below.

   a. Who wants to come *into our hearts?* _____

   b. Who can answer Jesus' voice? _____

   c. What does Jesus want me to do? He wants me to let Him _____ *into my heart.*

   d. What will Jesus Christ do when I open the door of my heart? He will _____ in.

   e. Have you asked Jesus Christ to come *into your heart?* Are you a *Christian* now? ____Yes ____No

1

---

3. Jesus Christ came to *save* people who are (Luke 19:10) *Lost* means everyone who does not know Jesus as *Savior.*

4. Read Romans 3:23. Why are people *lost?* Because they have _____

5. Romans 6:23 says that *sin* "pays" or brings us _____. This means that *sin* separates *sinners* from God. *Sinners* will live in *hell* when they die. But, Jesus Christ gives *believers* the gift of *eternal life.* *Believers* will live in *heaven* when they die.

6. Romans 5:8 (TEB) says, "But _____," died for us while we were still

7. Find the Book of 1 John. It is near the end of the New Testament. 1 John is one of John's letters. It is not the same as the Book of John. Read 1 John 1:9 (TEB). "But if we _____ our *sins,* He will _____ our *sins*." *Confess* means to tell God we are *sinners.*

8. Isaiah 55:7 (TEB) says: "Evil people should stop being evil. They should stop thinking bad thoughts. . . . They should come to God, because He will freely *forgive* them." They must *repent* of their *sins.*

   a. Evil people must stop being _____.

   b. They must stop _____ bad thoughts.

   c. What will God do when we repent? He will _____ me.

9. Find Ephesians 2:8-9. Put an X in front of the correct answer. The way to be *saved* is:

   ____ a. I must do a lot of work.
   ____ b. I must try to *save* myself.
   ____ c. I must believe in Jesus Christ to *save* me.

10. Read Ephesians 2:10. We are to do _____ after we are *saved.* Do good works *save* us? ____Yes ____No

2

---

11. We learn to know the _____ through Jesus Christ. (John 14: 6, 9)

12. Read 1 John 5:13. *Believers* can _____ that they have *eternal life* now.

13. The person who believes in Jesus has *eternal* _____. This means I will live forever. I will live in _____ when I die. (John 6:47)

14. How do you know that you are a child of God? Tell how you know in your own words. _____.

15. Jesus has given new life to you. You are a child of God. Now, how can you grow as a *Christian*? Here are some important ways you can grow as a *Christian*.

    a. **Read your Bible every day.** Read Matthew 4:4. Then, read a chapter in the Book of John each day. These lessons have questions from the Book of John. Also, there are questions from other books in the Bible. Study the memory verse for each lesson. Memorize each one.

    b. **Pray every day.** Talk to God. There are no special words you must say. Talk to God as you talk to a good friend.

    c. **Go to church as often as you can.** Go to a church that preaches from the Bible. Go to a church that preaches about Jesus. You need to be with other *Christians*. They will help you live for Jesus.

    d. **Obey God.** Ask God to help you. He will tell you what you should do. He will speak to you through the Bible. He will speak to you in church. Ask yourself, "What would Jesus do?" The answer will help you obey God.

    e. **Witness to other people.** Tell someone else what Jesus Christ did for you. *Witness* to other people that you are now a *Christian*.

3

Now, you should understand better what a *Christian* is. This is only the start of your *Christian* life. There is more joy to come!

Word List

1. **believers** (*noun*): people who believe in Jesus Christ as their Savior; people who receive Jesus *into their hearts*; all people who are *Christians*.

2. **Christian** (*proper noun*): a person who *repents* of *sins* and believes in Jesus; a person who follows and obeys Jesus Christ.

3. **confess** (*verb*): tell God that you know you are a *sinner*; tell God about your *sins* and your evil thoughts and acts.

4. **eternal life** (*noun phrase*): the life that God gives; the life with God now and with Him forever in *heaven*.

5. **forgive** (*verb*): not punish someone for their bad thoughts and acts; (God *forgives* and forgets our *sins* when we *repent*.)

6. **heaven** (*noun*): the home of *Christians* after death.

7. **hell** (*noun*): the place where *sinners* are punished after death.

8. **into my heart, into our hearts** (*prepositional phrase*): in the inner person; in the center of people; (The heart includes the mind, will, and desires of a person.)

9. **lost** (*adjective*): not finding the way to God; without hope of *eternal life*; not knowing Jesus Christ as *Savior*.

10. **repent** (*verb*): ask God to *forgive sins*; turn away from *sin* and turn to God.

11. **save; saves** (*verb*): make free from *sin*; (Jesus Christ *saves* or cleans us of our *sins*. Therefore, He *saves* us from being punished in *hell*.)

12. **Savior** (*proper noun*): Jesus Christ; the One who *saves* us from *sin*.

13. **sin** (*verb*); **sins** (*noun*): do bad acts and think bad thoughts; not obeying God; bad thoughts or acts.

14. **sinner** (*noun*): a person who does not obey the laws of God; a person who *sins*.

15. **witness** (*verb*): tell people about Jesus Christ; tell what Jesus Christ has done for you.

4

APPENDIX H

Engel's Evangelistic Countdown

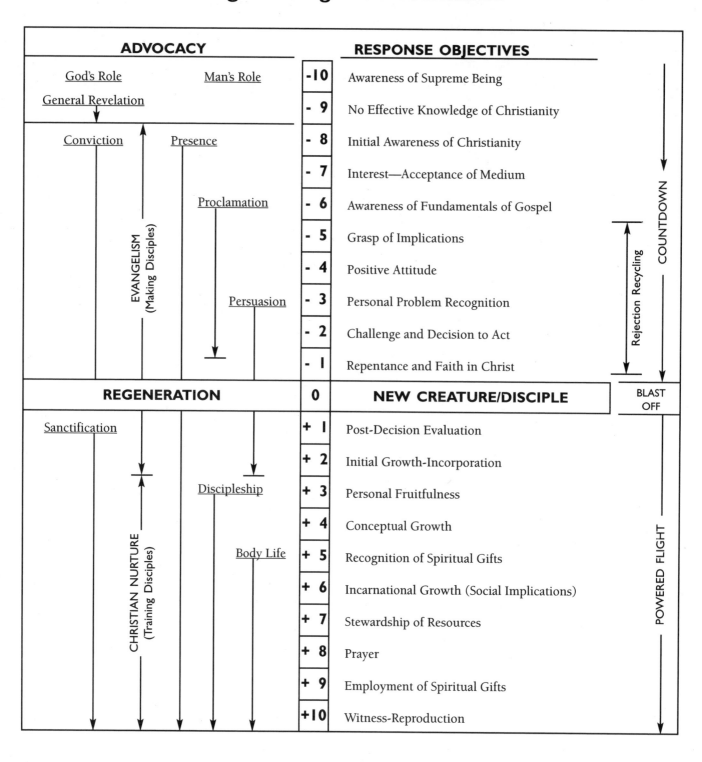

ADVOCACY			RESPONSE OBJECTIVES	
God's Role — General Revelation	**Man's Role**	-10	Awareness of Supreme Being	COUNTDOWN
		- 9	No Effective Knowledge of Christianity	
Conviction	Presence	- 8	Initial Awareness of Christianity	
		- 7	Interest—Acceptance of Medium	
	Proclamation	- 6	Awareness of Fundamentals of Gospel	
EVANGELISM (Making Disciples)		- 5	Grasp of Implications	Rejection Recycling
		- 4	Positive Attitude	
	Persuasion	- 3	Personal Problem Recognition	
		- 2	Challenge and Decision to Act	
		- 1	Repentance and Faith in Christ	
REGENERATION		**0**	**NEW CREATURE/DISCIPLE**	BLAST OFF
Sanctification		+ 1	Post-Decision Evaluation	POWERED FLIGHT
	Discipleship	+ 2	Initial Growth-Incorporation	
		+ 3	Personal Fruitfulness	
CHRISTIAN NURTURE (Training Disciples)	Body Life	+ 4	Conceptual Growth	
		+ 5	Recognition of Spiritual Gifts	
		+ 6	Incarnational Growth (Social Implications)	
		+ 7	Stewardship of Resources	
		+ 8	Prayer	
		+ 9	Employment of Spiritual Gifts	
		+10	Witness-Reproduction	

APPENDIX 1

Tips on Using a Gospel Tract

Gospel tracts are very useful visual tools in sharing our faith because they give:

- Something to focus on, not heightened emotions.
- Something to refer back to later when questions arise.
- Something for seekers to ask questions about while you are sharing the gospel.
- Something to make your memory better to share a clear, bold message.
- Something that allows ease in stopping and starting when witnessing gets stalled.
- Something small to assure seekers this is simple, short, and has an end.
- Something to help seekers see clearly where they are spiritually and where they can be.
- Something to help seekers know others are on the same journey; they are not alone.

Gospel tracts are very useful tools in keeping presenters focused on:

- Providing God's message clearly and humbly.
- Comparing our own experience with God's plan.
- Keeping presentations short, with few words, little detail, and few verses.
- Allowing seekers to choose for themselves where they are in relation to God.
- Following up steps after conversion (i.e., basic Bible study, prayer, tithing).

Transitional sentences prior to gospel tract use:

1. Sue [use name], you and I have been praying for _____. Where have you seen God at work?
2. Tom, you have asked me to pray for _____ but, I am wondering if you know for certain that the person you have been praying for knows Jesus Christ in a personal way? Would you explain how?
3. Sue, I know you have always gone to church. There was a time in my life when I thought that was enough, then someone showed me what had been missing from my spiritual life. May I show you?
4. Tom, do you ever feel that you cannot do enough to please others? I learned that what was most important was to obey God. May I show you how you can know this too?
5. Sue, I went to church as a young person, but I never knew what it meant to have peace with God. Have you ever felt that way?

Tips:

- Familiarize yourself with your tract before using it.
- Do not read every verse on each tract page. Be selective.
- Compare God's gift of eternal life as a gift your seeker needs to receive.
- Explain God has been calling your seeker for a long time.
- Thank God in prayer for having His hand on your seeker.
- Sign and date the tract as a reminder of the day of your seeker's conversion.
- Invite seekers to ask you questions.
- Select a tract that gives postconversion steps of discipleship and assurance.
- Listen to how your seeker has made personal attempts to be saved and has failed (often their failures are due to no knowledge of Christ, no challenge to holy living offered, no understanding of God, no confession of sin).

APPENDIX J

Resources

Tracts

Steps to Peace with God (gospel tract)
Billy Graham Evangelistic Association
P.O. Box 779
Minneapolis, MN 55440-0779
1-800-487-0433

AD/BC (Mission America tract)
Mission America Lighthouse Movement
5666 Lincoln Dr., No. 100
Edina, MN 55436-1673
1-612-912-0001
www.lighthousemovement.com

Yours for Life
American Tract Society
FYFL
1-888-556-0MAA

Four Spiritual Laws (gospel tract)
Campus Crusade for Christ
NewLife Publications
100 Sunport Ln.
Orlando, FL 32809

Church Visitation Resources

Personal Evangelism Training
Order No.: S-1991
Beacon Hill Press of Kansas City
1-800-877-0700 or orders@nph.com

Becoming a Contagious Christian
By Bill Hybels
Order No.: 031-021-0089
Zondervan Publishing House
1-800-727-3480

People Sharing Jesus
Broadman Holman Publishers
1-800-251-3225

Church Training Resources

Houses of Prayer Everywhere (provides training, re-
     sources, and ongoing support)
P.O. Box 141312
Grand Rapids, MI 49514

1-800-217-5200
Fax: 616-791-9926

Alpha Course Evangelism
Training Curriculum
1-800-WHYALPHA
www.AlphaNA.com

Mainstay Church Resources
David Mains
Box 30
Wheaton, IL 60189
1-800-224-2735

Crusade Evangelism and the Local Church
Sterling Huston
Billy Graham Evangelistic Association
Wheaton, IL 60189

HOPE Ministries Church Lighthouse Kit
HOPE Ministries
1-800-217-5200
info@hopeministries.org

Praying for You
Howard Tryon
P.O. Box 35834
Phoenix, AZ 85069
1-602-863-3400

House of Prayer: Developing a Church Prayer Strategy
Prayer Transformation Ministries
1-612-278-1717

Draw People to God Before Conversion

Knowing God
Living the Natural Way
1-816-339-5569

Jesus Video Project
24600 Arrowhead Springs Rd.
San Bernardino, CA 92414
1-888-537-8736

Better than Imagined
Order No.: 083-411-8173
Beacon Hill Press of Kansas City
1-800-877-0700 or orders@nph.com

How to Live Forever
Order No.: 084-233-3452
Tyndale House Publishers
Wheaton, IL 60189

Alpha Conference
Alpha North America
P.O. Box 5209
FDR Station
New York, NY 10150-5209
1-888-949-2574

Presenting the Gospel with Tough Questions

Bridgebuilder Handbook
Luis Palau Evangelistic Association
P.O. Box 1173
Portland, OR 97207
1-503-614-1500

Billy Graham Christian Worker's Handbook
WorldWide Publications
1303 Henepin Ave.
Minneapolis, MN 55403

Life: Any Questions?
Order No.: 084-991-2121
Word Publishing

Follow-up of New Converts

Basic Bible Studies (sets available for all ages)
Beacon Hill Press of Kansas City
1-800-877-0700 or orders@nph.com

Beginning with Christ
Order No.: 089-109-1599
NavPress
P.O. Box 35002
Colorado Springs, CO 80935
1-800-955-4432

Going On with Christ
Order No.: 990-073-2618
NavPress
P.O. Box 35002
Colorado Springs, CO 80935
1-800-955-4432

Conserve the Converts
Order No.: 083-410-4113
Beacon Hill Press of Kansas City
1-800-877-0700 or orders@nph.com

Personal Follow-up Set
Campus Crusade for Christ
1-800-729-4351

Growing Strong in God's Family
NavPress
P.O. Box 35002
Colorado Springs, CO 80935
1-800-955-4432

The New Believer's Growth Bible
Harvest Ministries
P.O. Box 4000
Riverside, CA 92514-4000

Other Personal Witnessing Resources

Evangelism in Everyday Life
Order No.: 083-411-7185
Beacon Hill Press of Kansas City
1-800-877-0700 or orders@nph.com

How to Share Your Faith
Order No.: 084-233-3452
Tyndale House Publishers
Wheaton, IL 60189

You Can Be a Witnessing Christian
Order No.: 083-411-3759
Beacon Hill Press of Kansas City
1-800-877-0700 or orders@nph.com

A Teen's Guide to Sharing My Faith
Order No.: 083-411-3848
Beacon Hill Press of Kansas City
1-800-877-0700 or orders@nph.com

Lighthouse Christmas Party Packets
Neighborly Evangelism
1-800-838-4368

Good Witnessing New Testaments

Beyond 99
Thomas Nelson Inc.
1-888-800-2767
contact Rev. Brent Regis
E-mail: info@rbmi.org

The Campus Prayer Handbook for Students
LINC Ministries
1-503-266-9914
lincministries@compuserve.com

Lighthouse Bible Studies

Your Home a Lighthouse
Order No.: 089-109-1270
NavPress
P.O. Box 35001
Colorado Springs, CO 80935

Evangelistic Web Sites

Christian Answers
www.christiananswers.net

Christian Apologetics and Research Ministry
www.carm.org

Who is Jesus?
www.whoisjesus.org

NeedHim
www.needhim.org

The Good News
www.thegoodnews.org

Ten Reasons to Believe
www.gospel.com/rbc/10rsn.home

Outreach Alert
www.outreachalert.org

Evangelism Toolbox
www.evangelismtoolbox.com

Mission America Lighthouse
www.lighthousemovement.com

Alpha Course Evangelism Training
www.AlphaNA.com

Mission America Materials

The Lighthouse Movement Handbook
Order No.: 157-673-6334
Multnomah Publishers
P.O. Box 1720
Sisters, Oregon

HOPE Ministries Personal Lighthouse Kit
1-800-271-5200
info@hopeministries.org

Developing a Prayer, Care, Share Lifestyle
1-800-271-5200
info@hopeministries.org

Light Your Street Resource Kit
1-800-423-5054, ext. 273

Lighthouse Christmas Party Packets
Neighborly Evangelism
1-800-838-4360

Spiritual Gifts Survey

Finding Your Ministry
By Raymond W. Hurn
Order No.: 083-410-6094
Beacon Hill Press of Kansas City
1-800-877-0700 or orders@nph.com

Sanctification Resources

All for His Glory Bible Study Series
    Filled with His Glory
    Transformed by His Glory
    Behold His Glory
Beacon Hill Press of Kansas City
1-800-877-0700 or orders@nph.com

A Layman's Guide to Sanctification
By H. Ray Dunning
Order No.: 083-411-3872
Beacon Hill Press of Kansas City
1-800-877-0700 or orders@nph.com

The Cycle of Victorious Living
By Earl and Hazel Lee
Order No.: 083-410-2757
Beacon Hill Press of Kansas City
1-800-877-0700 or orders@nph.com

Living in the Power of the Spirit
By Charles "Chic" Shaver
Order No.: S-250
Beacon Hill Press of Kansas City
1-800-877-0700 or orders@nph.com

APPENDIX K

Lighting the Way Leader's Guide
for Pastors and Leaders

You may have registered to become a Lighthouse as a family, an individual, or part of your local church. Since then, you may have wondered how you could become a more effective Lighthouse in your neighborhood, school, or workplace. *Lighting the Way* will help you in your journey of becoming a Lighthouse.

If you have not yet registered as a Lighthouse, you can become a part of this historic move of God by registering at <www.lighthouse-movement.com or by calling toll free 1-888-323-1210. By joining the Lighthouse Movement you will be informed of resources, events, and cooperative citywide efforts that will transform our nation through Jesus Christ. God wants us to work together to demonstrate the love and cooperation the world knows not of. He has commanded us to do so. The fact is, we work better together as a team than we do separately. Get registered today.

If your church would like to register to become a Lighthouse church, the steps are outlined at <www.lighthousemovement.com>. By using the suggested guidelines, you can insure your Lighthouse church will be what God has planned for you.

About the Material

Workbook Format

Historically, witnessing materials tend to be heavy on inspiration and teaching and light on the step-by-step how-tos. Books often teach methods without applying principles into daily experience. We can choose to read for years on the subject of witnessing and never apply one skill, thus being poor stewards of the time He has given us to accomplish His work. *Lighting the Way* contains easy self-study steps to eliminate lengthy, often costly, training. Any believer can use *Lighting the Way*. The daily format of Scripture reading, short text, and prayer, care, and share action steps fit busy lifestyles and offer easy review when used in a Sunday School or other small-group setting. By focusing on prayer, care, and share principles everyone can participate. Short daily formats break down large concepts into bite-size pieces with a sequential step-by-step process clearly defined for each participant. *Lighting the Way* is a complement to the growing national Lighthouse Movement, which endeavors to call all Christians to witnessing.

Ongoing Connection

If you will, provide my web site address <www.outreachalert.org> as a resource for answering questions participants may encounter in their witnessing, or to request prayer support.

Accountability Structure

The *Lighting the Way* accountability partner structure places high value on results over rhetoric. Participants may choose a prayer partner from their church group, or you may assign accountability partners. See the introduction for accountability partner guidelines.

Implementation

Lighting the Way is designed to be maintained with minimal time, effort, and cost. It is good to have a designated church *Lighting the Way* leader or leaders to implement the suggested steps below. Only 5 to 10 minutes of a Sunday School class or other regular group meeting will sustain the goals of the 90-day journey outlined below. See "Pastor's Letter" (Appendix L) for implementation details.

Rationale

Many churches do not have, or cannot sustain, church evangelism visitation teams when only a small percentage of their membership participate in the expansion of the church. *Lighting the Way* is unique in that it allows all believers to exercise the roles God has ordained for them in the witnessing process. At the conclusion of the 90-day journey, participants will know if their strongest gifts from God fall into either prayer or caring or sharing of the gospel. While they will do all three, participants will find it natural to implement one or two easily. Leaders should find ways to encourage and highlight each participant's unique gifts in prayer, care, or share areas. Anyone who sincerely commits to *Lighting the Way* will grow spiritually and skillfully. *Lighting the Way* dispels the myth that conversion numbers "earned" is more important than God's *process* of sharing. For those not gifted in evangelism, *Lighting the Way* let's them know they can be effective witnesses regardless. *Lighting the Way* helps rid believers of the quiet, unspoken guilt of not sharing their faith effectively. It helps them start somewhere and keep going into a Christian lifestyle, not a program. *Lighting the Way* helps participants actively demonstrate their own thankfulness to God for saving them by sharing it with others. The blessings of God will rest upon believers who faithfully share the gospel as Jesus commanded.

Why the Need for a Workbook?

Most evangelism tools are hard for many believers to navigate. When a method is introduced, it may be difficult to know how it can specifically apply in your life. *Lighting the Way* takes participants through a step-by-step process of *applying* principles so they do not have to figure it out. This enables participants to direct more energy toward seekers. Since 95 percent of most Christians today have never shared their faith with an unsaved person to bring them to Christ, these other methods, while worthy, have not demonstrated broad effectiveness. *Lighting the Way* concentrates on the principles to be applied, not on the method. Each page of this study is designed to move the participant through selective steps and topics of growth, which allow for an evaluation of their progress, and accountability to ensure growth. Self-study eliminates the need for lengthy professional training.

Objectives Are Simple

1. Participants will be applying the scriptural truth along with prayer, care, and share principles that bring others closer to Jesus Christ.

2. Participants will set their own study/application pace without the aid of formal training.

3. Participants will be held accountable to a prayer partner to validate their progress.

4. Participants will keep their eyes off of the conversion outcomes, preferring to focus on the "process" as the measure of success, not the number of conversions.

5. Participants will choose to redo, review, or refresh the *Lighting the Way* workbook prayer, care, share guidelines as necessary to ensure ultimate success in skill development, lifestyle adjustments, and witnessing growth.

Growth

Lighting the Way participants are expected to grow in the following areas:

1. Learning key skills to effective witnessing

2. Applying key skills on a consistent basis

3. Evaluating progress of skills by God's standard, not ours

4. Altering negative attitudes that may have restrained growth

5. Adjusting personal schedules to reflect new priorities, placing a higher value on pleasing God than oneself

Sample Weekly Plan for Leaders, Accountability Partners, or Small Groups

1. Choose a preexisting meeting time to avoid adding more to participants' schedules and to make it routine each week.

2. Ask each participant to spend 5 to 10 minutes alone before a regular meeting. Ask:

- What are answers to one or two questions from the day 6 review summary?

- What new witnessing skills are you learning?

- What witnessing progress are you making from God's viewpoint?

- How are your attitudes improving concerning witnessing?

● Where do you and your seekers need prayer this week? Then *pray.*

3. Practice the lessons on personal testimony formulation and gospel presentation (weeks 9 and 10). Spend more class time as needed. Taking time for participants to share these with the class would be beneficial for sharing the gospel with ease, clarity, and assurance.

APPENDIX L

Letter to Pastors and
Lighting the Way Leaders

Dear Pastor:

Thank you for your willingness to use *Lighting the Way* in the evangelism ministry of your church. You surely share the heart of most pastors that all believers in your congregation will be effective in sharing their faith in Jesus Christ. A look at church staffing indicates most churches hire either a music or teen minister (ministering directly to 10 percent of the total body) after their senior pastor. This leaves a ratio of 1-200 parishioners in the direct leadership of the total church body under the senior pastor. Within this hefty ratio, the largest portion of the vision of the church, witnessing is executed by the pastor alone or left undone due to overload.

Most churches do not hire a staff evangelist to equip believers in Kingdom expansion ministry. Consequently, even though on paper the mission of the church may be the Great Commission, in actuality the Kingdom expansion-equipping ministry is weak in most churches. It has been reported that less than 2 percent (see *Conserve the Converts*) of any given congregation actively participate in the evangelism ministry within the church. Since the Bible calls for the priesthood of the believers to work as harvesters, what is happening with the other 98 percent? You have taken the first step in reversing this tide. You have chosen to strengthen your Kingdom expansion ministry. Obedience in this area will encourage numerical and spiritual growth. For average churches who have pastoral turnover every two to three years, this also gives continuity of mission/vision in ongoing church ministry.

Your church's mission/vision will be enhanced by encouraging all believers in Kingdom expansion ministry on some level. Rom. 12:1-8 reminds us that each believer is gifted uniquely for the task. This is a team effort. *Lighting the Way* implementation is easy and cost-effective. Building Great Commission disciples is eternally

profitable. Here are some sequential steps to help you as you lead your congregation in *Lighting the Way* implementation:

Leader Implementation Steps

1. Prayerfully commit to church growth through the priesthood of the believers.

2. Prayerfully hand-pick a church Great Commission leader. (Someone with the gifts of administration, evangelism, teaching, motivating, speaking, and doctrinal understanding are good starters. Have them work with Sunday School teachers and other leaders.)

3. Commit to modeling *Lighting the Way* principles yourself and oversee your Great Commission leader.

4. Introduce and cast vision for your key leaders in prayer, care, share/*Lighting the Way* principles

5. Register your church as a national Lighthouse church at <www.lighthousemovement.com> or call toll free 1-888-323-1210.

6. Deliver five to six sermons on "doing the work of the evangelist" prior to *Lighting the Way* use.

7. Provide *Lighting the Way* registration forms in all classes, bulletins, and newsletters.

8. Lead a Lighthouse Commissioning service and distribute *Lighting the Way* books.

9. Assist in *Lighting the Way* participants' selection of accountability partners as needed.

10. Begin ongoing five-minute *Lighting the Way* testimonials in worship services and classes.

11. Maintain ongoing Lighthouse/*Lighting the Way* bulletin and newsletter sections with interesting stories and tips.

12. Highlight numbers of Lighthouse participants along with regular tithe and attendance reports.

13. Place a Lighthouse Chart with your

Lighting the Way participants added as part of your Lighthouse church team.

14. Recognize *Lighting the Way* participants with Lighthouse certificates, pins, public awards.

15. Send your *Lighting the Way* success stories to Mission America Lighthouse Hotline.

16. In all ways make *Lighting the Way* Lighthouse participation "the" ministry for involvement.

17. Keep the light burning in your Lighthouses with these ongoing ideas:

- Personal testimonies during worship services every Sunday for three minutes. (Have participants fill out a form with testimony to ensure this is kept short.)
- Church bulletin with reminders (materials from study material, such as the thought for the week).
- Newsletter feature each month on Lighthouse/*Lighting the Way* News (using stories submitted).
- Commissioning Service (for newly registered Lighthouses).
- Pastoral appreciation awards/plaques (i.e., Lighthouse lapel pins, certificates).
- Pastoral prayer (include ongoing prayer for Lighthouses and seekers).
- Pastoral sermons on the importance of sharing our faith (ongoing during 90 days).

- *Lighting the Way* participant/seekers who come to Christ recognition (Lighthouse altar).
- Bulletin Board (one-word benefits of doing *Lighting the Way*/participant name [i.e., Fulfilled]) (other words could be selected, such as *exhilaration, thankful, motivated, blessed, hopeful, privilege, guilt-free, confident, influential, adventure, positive, enthusiastic, obedient, satisfaction, energized, godly*).
- Prayer chain for seeker needs and praise over conversions.

18. More leader's guide tips will be made available on the Outreach Alert web site at <www.outreachalert.org> each month. E-mail your ideas, and we will post those also.

Pastor, as God has called you to equip, train, and give vision to "the work of the evangelist" within the spiritual lives of your congregation, it is our belief that you will find *Lighting the Way* effective in bringing a greater number of your congregation to obedience in this area of their walk with Christ. Your congregation will grow in many ways (even in tithing and leadership) as a result of their obedience in this often feared area of being a good disciple. May God add His blessings upon you as you lead your flock.

Yours in Christian service,
Mary Marr

Bibliography

Frizzell, Naomi. "Christian Radio and the Great Commission." Mission America and the Lighthouse Movement, May 2000.

Haan, Cornell, comp. *Lighthouse Movement Handbook.* Sisters, Oreg.: Multnomah, 1999.

Laurie, Greg. *How to Share Your Faith.* Wheaton, Ill.: Tyndale House, 1999.

Peterson, Jim. *Evangelism as a Lifestyle.* Colorado Springs: NavPress, 1982.

Reflecting God Study Bible. Grand Rapids: Zondervan, 2000.

Shaver, Charles "Chic." *Conserve the Converts.* Kansas City: Beacon Hill Press of Kansas City, 1998.